SELF-HELP EMOTIONAL ABUSE RECOVERY

A Book About Emotional Abuse in All Areas of Life
with a 30-Day Workbook for Deep Transformation

JULIANNA KENT

SELF-HELP EMOTIONAL ABUSE RECOVERY

A Book About Emotional Abuse in All Areas of Life
with a 30-Day Workbook for Deep Transformation

2025

This book is not just a collection of incredible facts, but a true guide to a world of knowledge presented with humor and fun. Forget about boring encyclopedias and dull books — in this one, every fact will surprise and make you laugh! Why stare at screens when you can dive into a captivating world full of fascinating discoveries and exciting adventures?

Each chapter is filled with not only interesting facts but also interactive activities for the whole family, making reading even more fun. This book proves that reading can be not only educational but also enjoyable and the perfect way to spend time with your loved ones. Read, laugh, and have a great time together, discussing the most unexpected facts and completing fun activities.

CONTENTS

DEDICATION

Greetings, dear reader!

My name is Julianna Kent, and I'm a psychologist. My work is to help people who find themselves in toxic relationships and are learning to trust themselves and the world again. Over the years, I have met many women and men: some recognized they were in abusive relationships but didn't know how to escape, while others didn't notice the manipulation and control for a long time, gradually losing confidence in themselves. People often think the problem is with them, that they are too sensitive or that this is just how things are in any relationship. But that is far from the truth.

I decided to write this book so that everyone could see, understand, and recognize abuse in their own lives. The purpose of this book is not only to help identify toxic relationships but also to provide clear guidance on how to break free from the vicious cycle of abuse. I understand that psychology can be difficult for many, so I will strive to explain everything in simple language. There will be no complicated terminology or heavy theory here. Instead, I focus on practical advice and real-life examples that you can easily apply in your own life.

Special attention is given to the importance of not only recognizing abuse but also knowing what to do next. This book covers all aspects of life: relationships with partners, colleagues, parents, and friends. We will discuss how abuse can manifest in different areas of your life, and how you can learn to set boundaries and respect yourself.

I particularly want to highlight the 30-day workbook included in the book. This tool will help you restore your emotional state, learn to forgive yourself, take care of yourself, cope with the consequences of abuse, and start moving toward a better life. Step by step, day by day, if you work on yourself, you will regain your confidence and strength.

I hope this book becomes not just a guide but a roadmap, showing the way to a life free of abuse. This is your chance to understand that you deserve respect, love, and happiness. Don't delay your introduction to this book—start reading now, because life is short, and each of us deserves to live our best version.

With love and support,
Julianna Kent!

CHAPTER 1
WHAT IS EMOTIONAL ABUSE?

Greetings, dear reader. I'm glad that you've decided to open this book. This is the first step towards realizing your situation and, most importantly, towards healing from the pain caused by abusive relationships. You might be wondering: "Do I have this problem? Is this really emotional abuse, or am I just overreacting?" These questions are completely normal. We often doubt ourselves, especially when it comes to emotions and relationships. But let's figure it out together.

It's important to understand what exactly is happening to you. Why? Let's say you have a stomach ache. And you don't know if it's your stomach or pancreas, so it's unclear what medicine will help, and you can't prescribe effective treatment. Without knowledge, it's easy to get confused. So, let's start with the basics. And don't worry, the theory won't be boring. We will break everything down with examples that will help you better understand what emotional abuse is.

ABUSE: IT AFFECTS EVERYONE

Emotional abuse, or abuse, also known as psychological abuse or moral pressure, can affect anyone. Sometimes even a seemingly harmless phrase can be the first sign of it. Imagine someone saying, "What a stupid thing you came up with." For one person, it might go unnoticed, but for another, it becomes the reason to start doubting themselves.

Everyone has a different sensitivity threshold. Some are sensitive, and even a few hurtful phrases can make someone retreat into themselves, fall into depression, or start doubting their own worth. Meanwhile, another person, the "tough nut," brushes off hurtful words and quickly forgets unpleasant moments. And that's okay. We're all different. That's why this book will help you fit the information to your own life and understand if emotional abuse is present in your life and, if it is, how it specifically manifests for you.

Abuse can occur not only in romantic relationships but also in other areas of life. Sometimes the source of emotional pain can be the most unexpected people. Let's look at the main situations where it can manifest:

In the Family: Emotional abuse can come from parents, siblings, or even more distant relatives. For example, a mother constantly devalues you by saying, "You'll never achieve anything," or a brother uses sarcasm to hurt you, "You always do everything wrong."

In Relationships: A partner can demonstrate both obvious and hidden forms of abuse. It could be sharp comments, manipulation, or control over your actions. For example, a partner demands to know every step you take or says, "If you really loved me, you'd stop seeing your friends."

At Work: A boss might devalue your contribution, saying, "Is this all you're capable of?" A colleague might spread rumors or deliberately ignore your ideas. These situations not only destroy professional self-esteem but also put pressure on your emotional stability.

Neighbors or Acquaintances: Sometimes, abuse comes from those with whom we don't have close relationships. For example, a neighbor constantly criticizes your lifestyle: "You're too loud, you don't belong here" — creating a constant background of stress.

These examples show that emotional abuse can come from anyone, anywhere. We will learn how to recover from all these types, as any form of emotional pain requires attention and self-care.

So now you know that almost everyone can experience abuse, and it can manifest in different areas of life. It's time to learn about its main forms:

GASLIGHTING

Gaslighting is when someone makes you doubt your own reality.

How it manifests:

- In Relationships: A partner says, "You're making it all up, that never happened," when you remind them of their promise.
- At Work: A colleague claims you forgot to send an important email, even though you're sure you did it.
- In the Family: A parent insists, "You've always been ungrateful," making you feel guilty without reason.

MANIPULATION

Manipulation often targets your emotions.

How it manifests:

- In Relationships: "If you loved me, you wouldn't argue with me."
- At Work: A boss threatens, "If you don't work overtime, I'll find someone who will."
- In the Family: "You owe me help, after all, I'm your mother."

CONTROL

Control involves restricting your freedom.

How it manifests:

- In Relationships: A partner forbids you from seeing friends or controls your finances.

- At Work: A boss insists that you always respond to messages, even on weekends.
- In the Family: Parents dictate who you should socialize with or where to live, even if you're an adult.

DEVALUATION

When your feelings and achievements are dismissed.

How it manifests:

- In Relationships: "You're overreacting, it's not a big deal."
- At Work: "Your project isn't important, you should focus on something more useful."
- In the Family: "You've never achieved anything, and when I was your age, I..."

ISOLATION

An abuser might try to distance you from your loved ones.

How it manifests:

- In Relationships: "Your friends are a bad influence on you. Stop hanging out with them."
- At Work: Colleagues deliberately don't invite you to important meetings.
- Neighbors: Constant complaints about you can make you feel unwelcome.

This is all theory, but let's look at specific examples of how different types of emotional abuse manifest in real life. Let me introduce you to two characters — Emily and Sarah. Throughout the book, they will help us navigate all the nuances. Perhaps you will recognize yourself or someone you know in their stories. Remember: there's nothing shameful about seeking answers and help. It's a sign of strength, not weakness. Let's dive in.

Emily's Story: Toxic Relationship with Her Partner

Emily has been dating Matt for five years. At the beginning, their relationship seemed perfect: he gave her flowers, wrote sweet notes, and said she was the woman of his dreams. But gradually, his behavior changed.

Matt began controlling her every move. When Emily wanted to meet up with her friends, he'd say, "Why do you need them? You'd rather stay home, I miss you." She gave in to avoid conflict. Later came demeaning comments: "You don't understand anything about this," or "You always do everything wrong."

When Emily tried to share her feelings, he responded, "You're too sensitive. Stop making a big deal out of nothing." Her confidence began to fade. She increasingly doubted her feelings, decisions, and ability to perceive things correctly.

Emily found herself in a situation where her freedom was restricted, and her self-esteem was constantly undermined. This type of abuse can be described as a mix of control, devaluation, and gaslighting.

Sarah's Story: Toxic Work Environment

Sarah is a successful graphic designer. Her boss, Mr. Harper, seems friendly, but his behavior often crosses professional boundaries.

Every time Sarah offers ideas, Mr. Harper says, "Interesting, but this is too complex for you." In meetings, he publicly points out her mistakes, even when they weren't her fault: "You should have foreseen this, was that really that difficult?" Such comments make Sarah feel incompetent.

Additionally, Mr. Harper likes to manipulate his employees' emotions. When Sarah refuses to stay overtime without pay, he says, "If you don't want to help the team, then success in the company doesn't matter to you." This forces her to work more than she can handle.

Sarah begins to notice her professional confidence decreasing, and thoughts about work make her anxious.

WHAT DO THESE STORIES HAVE IN COMMON?

In both cases, there's an attempt to suppress the other person, make them doubt themselves, and make them comply. Emily's relationship with Matt and Sarah's with Mr. Harper are both based on manipulation and control, although they manifest differently. Emotional abuse can be both overt and subtle, but its goal is always the same — to establish power over another person.

It's important to remember: if you feel overwhelmed, humiliated, or helpless in your relationship with anyone — whether a partner, colleague, or boss — your feelings are real, and they deserve attention.

In the following chapters, we'll explore why it's so difficult to break this cycle and what can be done to start moving forward.

CHAPTER 2
WHERE IS THE LINE BETWEEN ABUSE AND LIFE SITUATIONS?

When someone starts to learn about emotional abuse, its types, forms, and mechanisms, it might seem like abuse is everywhere in our surroundings. Every unpleasant situation, every harsh phrase, or conflict begins to feel like moral violence.

Someone pushed you on the subway and rudely said, "Watch where you're going!" — is that abuse?
Parents raised their voices at their child because they ran into the street — is that abuse?

A friend made a joke, but it made you uncomfortable — is that moral pressure?

A husband and wife argue from time to time — does that mean their relationship is toxic?

So, should we live in complete isolation to avoid all this? Of course not.

In this chapter, we'll explore the difference between abuse and ordinary conflicts, and where to draw the line between a one-time unpleasant situation and a systemic destruction of a person's identity.

ABUSE IS A SYSTEM, NOT AN ISOLATED INCIDENT
The key difference between emotional abuse and an ordinary conflict is that abuse happens regularly and predictably.

A good example can be seen in the film *Sleepers* (1996), where the main characters were systematically tormented in a correctional facility during their childhood. Their abusers didn't just show aggression once, they did it methodically, creating an atmosphere of constant fear and helplessness. This shows that abuse is not just an argument or conflict, but a long-term suppression and manipulation of a person.

Another vivid example is the film *Enough* (2002) starring Jennifer Lopez. It tells the story of a woman who marries what seems to be the perfect man, but soon he begins to control her, humiliate her, and use physical violence. The film demonstrates how the abuser gradually destroys the victim's self-esteem and how hard it is to find the strength to leave. This highlights an important point: abuse is not just a series of occasional conflicts, but a systemic suppression of one person by another.

The key difference between emotional abuse and an ordinary conflict is that abuse happens regularly and predictably.

◆ Conflict is part of human relationships. Everyone argues from time to time, gets irritated, and might say something unpleasant. In healthy relationships, after a conflict, reconciliation follows, both sides can discuss the situation, reach a compromise, and learn from it.

◆ Abuse is a recurring pattern. One person consistently devalues, controls, or humiliates the other, using psychological pressure.

To make this clearer, let's look at these concepts through the examples of Sarah and Emily.

✔ *Emily is friends with a colleague who sometimes makes awkward jokes. One day she said, "You're taking too long on this project; everyone jokes that you're the slowest here." Emily felt uncomfortable and calmly explained to her friend that such words hurt her. The colleague apologized, promised not to say that again, and kept her word — this is not abuse.*

Now, let's look at a different situation with Sarah.

✘ *Sarah works with a boss who systematically mocks her in meetings: "Oh, here's Sarah again! Let's see what she has to surprise us with today." When she says it bothers her, he responds, "Come on, it's just a joke!" These situations repeat again and again, and Sarah starts feeling less confident — this is abuse.*

ABUSE IS INTENTIONAL SUPPRESSION, NOT JUST EMOTIONS

Emotions are a natural part of the human experience, and not every outburst of anger or irritation is abuse. Parents might shout at a child if they run into the street, or a partner might snap after a tough day, but that doesn't make them abusers. It's important to consider the context and frequency of these situations. If this happens occasionally and the person later realizes their mistake, apologizes, and changes their behavior, it's not considered emotional abuse. However, if shouting, humiliation, or suppression becomes systematic, and requests to stop are ignored — then it's abuse.

✔ A parent, in irritation, shouts at their child when they break a mug. A few minutes later, they calm down, explain they overreacted, and say they love them — this is not abuse.

✘ A parent constantly tells their child they are clumsy,

useless, and "nothing will come of them." When the child gets upset, the parent responds: "Why are you upset? Who else will tell you the truth if not your father?" — this is abuse.

✓ A friend forgot about your agreement to meet and didn't reply to your message. When you asked what happened, she apologized and promised to be more attentive — this is not abuse.

✗ A friend constantly ignores your requests, and when you get upset, she says: "Oh, here you go again with your drama. Can you relax for once?" — this is abuse.

These examples show that one-time emotional outbursts are not abuse if the person recognizes their mistakes and corrects their behavior. Abuse is a recurring pattern of behavior that destroys the victim's personality.

Also, when examining the difference between moral violence and just conflict, it's important to consider whether personal boundaries are being violated.

Sometimes people can be rude, irritated, or short-tempered. For example, a cashier might respond coldly, a colleague might say something sharp, or a friend might make a joke that makes you uncomfortable. This can hurt, but if it happens once and doesn't repeat systematically, it's not considered abuse.

An abuser regularly and intentionally breaks boundaries, using words or actions to suppress the other person. If you say, "I don't like it when you do that," and the response is "You're making it all up," "Stop dramatizing," or "I don't care" — that's already a sign of abuse. The abuser continues to push, even when you ask them to stop, making you feel guilty or petty.

LIVING WITHOUT ABUSE DOESN'T MEAN LIVING IN ISOLATION

It's important to understand that living without abuse doesn't mean living without conflicts. It's impossible to completely avoid unpleasant situations, but you can learn to distinguish between healthy disagreements and emotional violence.

Abuse is intentional, repeated suppression of a person.

Conflicts are a natural part of human relationships, and in a healthy environment, they are resolved with respect for each other's boundaries.

You are not obliged to tolerate violence, but you shouldn't see it where it doesn't exist either. Balance is the key to healthy perception of reality. I truly hope that this book helps you find that balance.

CHAPTER 3
THE CYCLE OF VIOLENCE

EMOTIONAL ABUSE: MORE COMPLEX THAN IT SEEMS

"Emotional abuse" — this phrase sounds frightening. For most people, it conjures up an image of one person shouting, waving their arms, while the other cries, trying to defend themselves, but can't. As we already know, emotional abuse can be much more subtle. It's not always loud arguments or obvious insults. Sometimes, it's just seemingly harmless comments, sarcastic reproaches, or controlling behavior masked as care.

This is why many people don't realize they are in an abusive relationship. "Well, yes, my husband sometimes loses his temper, but he's stressed at work," "Yes, my boss often criticizes me, but that's his job," "My parents might be rude, but they only want the best for me." The victim starts to justify the abuser: they had a bad day, they're nervous... But the truth is, emotional abuse has its structure, its cycle. It's not just random bursts of irritation, but a recurring scenario that pulls you in and destroys you.

THE ROLLER COASTER OF ABUSE

To better understand how this process works, imagine yourself on a roller coaster. You're climbing up, your heart is racing in anticipation, adrenaline pumping through your veins. You're filled with joy, excitement, the sensation of flying. And suddenly — a sharp drop, your stomach lurches, your chest tightens with fear, and all you can do is hold on and wait for the ride to end.

This is how abusive relationships work.

They begin with a "rise." The abuser may be incredibly charming, attentive, and tender. It's the "honeymoon" phase: you're surrounded by compliments, care, promises. You feel like you've found someone who understands you, values you, loves you like no one ever has before.

But then comes the drop. Gradually, irritation, reproaches, and criticism appear. At first, they're rare, minor, barely noticeable, but then they become more frequent. Love turns into control, care into neglect, support into pressure. And before you know it, you're not sure whether you're being treated the way you should be. You try to "guess the mood," avoiding anger, walking on eggshells to avoid triggering a storm.

Then comes the "plunge" — the moment of abuse. It could be shouting, accusations, ignoring, or gaslighting. At this moment, the victim feels humiliated, empty, crushed. They don't understand what they did wrong, but they feel guilty.

But then comes the next phase — the rise again. The abuser apologizes. They say they didn't mean it, that they were just "tired," "snapped," or "worried about you." They become loving, attentive, and caring again. And the victim decides to stay because they believe, "This is the person I love! It was just a tough time... They're trying, so everything will get better!"

But just like on the roller coaster, the drop is inevitable. And the cycle starts again.

This recurring scenario is one of the reasons victims stay in such relationships. If the abuse happened continuously, without the "ups," it would be much easier to leave.

But the contrast between "love" and "humiliation" creates a strong dependency.

The mechanism of emotional roller coasters doesn't only manifest in personal relationships. Similar cycles can occur in other areas of life: at work, in friendships, even in relationships with neighbors.

People who haven't studied abuse in all its forms often wonder whether a certain situation is emotional violence. This is why we'll examine the "roller coaster" of abuse, i.e., the cyclical nature of abusive behavior, through concrete examples of our characters, Sarah and Emily.

Sarah: Roller Coasters at Work

Sarah works as a graphic designer. Her boss, Mr. Harper, on some days seems like the perfect boss. He praises her work: "You're my best specialist! This project would have failed without you." Sarah feels like a valuable part of the team. She's confident that she's respected.

But then something changes. Her boss becomes irritable. He starts dismissively commenting on her ideas: "Well, that's weak. Think harder." Or during a meeting, he might say, "It should have been done differently, but you don't listen, and you always have your own opinion."

Then comes the peak — he might shout at her or humiliate her in front of colleagues. Sarah feels worthless, useless, as though she's doing everything wrong.

But then the "honeymoon" phase returns. Harper apologizes, says, "Sorry, I just had a bad day, I appreciate your work." Sarah sighs with relief: "Well, he's good again, everything will be fine..."

And the cycle repeats again.

Emotional abuse at work is not just a "tough management

style," but a real problem that undermines confidence, decreases productivity, and damages mental health. When praise turns into humiliation and approval into criticism, the employee begins to live in constant tension, trying to "earn" good treatment, leaving no room for new ideas or insights. This cycle traps the person, making them doubt themselves and fear change. But it's important to remember: respect at work is not a bonus, but the norm. If work becomes a source of fear and anxiety, it might be time to consider whether it's worth sacrificing your peace of mind.

Now let's look at another situation involving Emily. Notice, the cyclical pattern is the same, only the people and life situations change.

Emily: Toxic Relationship with a Neighbor

Emily found herself on an emotional roller coaster in her interactions with her neighbor, Mrs. Wright. On some days, Mrs. Wright is very friendly: "Emily, I baked a cake, have some! We neighbors should help each other out." Emily feels comfortable and even grateful.

But a couple of days later, something changes. Mrs. Wright notices that Emily left her bicycle in the hallway and sharply says, "You always make a mess! How can you be so irresponsible?" Emily apologizes, moves the bike, thinking she just caught her neighbor in a bad mood.

But then the neighbor starts ignoring her, coldly turning away when they meet. Emily doesn't understand what she did wrong. She's bothered by this silent disapproval.

And suddenly, the "honeymoon" phase returns: "Oh, Emily, I'm so glad to see you! Let's sit down and have some tea!" Emily relaxes, thinking everything is fine.

But a week later, the discontent starts again: "You slam the door so loudly, what manners are these?!"

Emily feels trapped but can't completely ignore her neighbor since they live next door.

Emotional abuse can even be hidden in seemingly normal neighborly interactions. When friendliness turns into harsh reproaches, and warmth into cold silence, a person begins to feel guilty, even when they haven't done anything wrong. Emily fell into the classic trap: she tries to adjust, guess her neighbor's mood, but ends up playing the role of the "guilty one." These relationships drain her and make her doubt herself.

Emotional roller coasters are not just a series of good and bad days. It's an entire system, where the "honeymoon" phases alternate with pain, creating an illusion of hope. When warmth and care follow humiliation, a person clings to those rare moments, believing everything can still be fixed. This contrast is what makes abusive relationships so addictive — it seems that if you just "endure" a little longer, everything will be fine again.

But if the pain inevitably returns, then the problem isn't with you, but with the cycle itself. This raises the crucial question: if a relationship causes so much suffering, why is it so hard to leave?

WHY IS IT SO HARD TO LEAVE?

Statistics show that over 70% of people encounter emotional abuse in some form — at home, at work, in relationships, or in friendships. But only about 30% find the strength to change the situation: leave, set boundaries, start a new life. The other 70% remain in this state not because they are comfortable, but because they either don't realize they are experiencing emotional abuse or don't see a real way to change the situation. Many try to adapt, justify the behavior of those around them, or simply survive in these conditions, lacking the resources or support to get out.

Agree, 70% is quite a high number. So why not change your life? Why not leave an abusive partner, change a toxic job, set boundaries with a neighbor, or talk to your family and say directly: "I don't like this, it hurts me"?

It's all about human psychology. Everyone has their own reasons, fears, and attachments. Let's break down why people stay in emotionally destructive environments, even when they realize they are unhappy.

1. Hope for the Better

When a boss, after a week of criticism, suddenly praises you for your work, when a strict parent unexpectedly says they're proud of you, when an abusive partner becomes affectionate again — you believe it. You want to believe it. Because there were moments when things were good. And you think: Maybe I'm the problem? Maybe if I'm more patient, kinder, work harder, everything will get better?

At work, it might look like this: your boss constantly criticizes you, undermines your confidence, and creates an atmosphere of fear. But then, after a successful project, they say, "You actually are a capable employee." And suddenly, you forget all the bad things and feel the urge to prove your worth again.

In families, the situation is similar: toxic parents manipulate love, instill guilt, and create emotional dependence. If, as a child, you were told, "I did so much for you, and you're so ungrateful," then as an adult, it may be incredibly hard to walk away from a parent who continues to belittle, control, or emotionally suppress you.

2. Fear of Change and Loneliness

What if life without this person or this job is even worse? What if you can't handle it? Especially if you've been told for years that you're nothing without them:

- _"Where would you go? You won't survive without me."_
- _"You'll never find a better job."_

Abusers in all areas of life — partners, bosses, even family members — use fear as a tool of control. In the workplace, it's the fear of losing financial stability. In families, it's the fear of rejection. In relationships, it's the fear of never finding love again.

Studies show that about 48% of victims of emotional abuse hesitate to leave a relationship primarily due to fear of loneliness and financial instability. This is especially true for women raising children and for people whose jobs have become psychological traps.

3. Attachment and Dependency

You love them. Not the boss who humiliates you in front of everyone, but the one who once supported you in a tough moment. Not the parent who constantly criticizes, but the one who used to tell you bedtime stories. Not the husband who yells, but the one who once gave you flowers and looked at you with tenderness.

This is how psychological dependency works. The more you invest in a person or situation, the harder it is to let go.

- _"I've spent so many years at this job..."_
- _"He promised he would change."_
- _"I can't leave my parents — they need me."_

This is known as the "sunk cost fallacy"—the more effort you've put into a relationship (or a job), the harder it is to leave, even if it's making you unhappy.

4. Guilt and Shame

Sometimes, it feels like leaving would mean betraying them, abandoning them in a difficult moment. Or that no one would understand, that people would judge you:

- *"Others have it worse."*
- *"You're just ungrateful."*

If toxic parents told you as a child, "I raised you, now you owe me," then as an adult, setting boundaries or walking away can feel nearly impossible without overwhelming guilt.

In the workplace, this manifests as loyalty pressure:

- *"How can you leave now, when the company is struggling?"*

In personal relationships, it takes the form of emotional manipulation:

- *"After everything I've done for you, you're just going to leave me?"*

SO WHY DO PEOPLE STAY?

Every person's experience is different, and so are their reasons for staying in difficult situations.

For some, changing jobs is just another step, a matter of a few weeks. For others, the idea of job hunting, interviews, and adapting to a new team feels far more terrifying than enduring a toxic boss. Some people easily cut off relationships when they feel discomfort. Others hold on for years because the fear of the unknown is stronger than the pain they endure.

We are all different. We have different emotional resilience, life experiences, opportunities, and resources. Judging someone for staying in an abusive situation — whether in work, family, or relationships — is unfair. No one else has lived their life. No one knows what fears, hopes, or circumstances are shaping their choices.

But it's important to remember: there is always a way out. Even if it feels like there isn't. The more you understand how this cycle works, the more you recognize your emotions and needs, the closer you get to breaking free — and choosing yourself.

CHAPTER 4
THE IMPACT OF EMOTIONAL ABUSE

INVISIBLE SCARS: THE CONSEQUENCES OF EMOTIONAL ABUSE

We often cannot immediately recognize the destructive power of emotional abuse. Physical abuse is immediately visible — bruises, scrapes, tears. But emotional blows leave no marks on the skin, even though their impact can be much deeper and more painful. They destroy a person from within, gradually eroding their emotional state, mental health, self-esteem, and even physical well-being.

It's like an unnoticed crack in glass: at first, you don't pay attention to it, but with each day, it grows bigger until one day the glass shatters. The same happens with a person — if you live for a long time in an environment where you are suppressed, criticized, and manipulated, there will come a point when it feels like nothing inside you remains whole.

But recognizing the problem is the first step to solving it. Perhaps, after reading about the consequences of emotional abuse, you'll realize that what you've been enduring is actually not normal. Maybe this will push you to stop the roller coaster of abuse, stop waiting and hoping for external change, and finally realize: your life is too valuable to waste it on pain and destruction.

Emotional abuse undoubtedly destroys a person. However, while the connection between a boss's yelling and feelings of suppression can be traced, the physiological consequences often go unnoticed. We rarely think that constant headaches, stomach issues, or chronic fatigue could be the result of stress caused by toxic relationships, humiliation, or gaslighting.

As you read about the consequences, some may recognize themselves in these patterns — and that could be the trigger to initiate change. Others might think: "No, this doesn't happen to me." But when the next "drop" in the emotional roller coaster is especially painful, those words will resurface in memory, and realization will come. Therefore, information about consequences is important — it helps you see the hidden, recognize the problem, and stop enduring, because life is meant for happiness, not for survival.

EMOTIONAL AND PSYCHOLOGICAL CONSEQUENCES

Emotional and psychological health are closely connected. We group them together because emotional abuse initially affects feelings and then penetrates deeper into the psyche. The difference is that emotions are our immediate reactions: fear, anxiety, resentment, shame. Whereas the psyche is how these emotions gradually form our beliefs, behavior, and reactions to the world.

If emotional abuse lasts for a long time, it turns into psychological tension, destroys self-confidence, changes one's perception of reality, and can even lead to depression or anxiety disorders.

When a person undergoes constant pressure, criticism, and humiliation, they begin to doubt their own feelings and emotions. Here are some characteristic consequences:

- Chronic anxiety: You constantly expect something to happen, that you'll be hurt, humiliated, or devalued. This state doesn't turn off even in moments of rest.

- Feelings of guilt and shame: The abuser convinces the victim that all the problems are their fault. You begin to believe that you deserve such treatment.
- Feeling of loneliness: Many victims of emotional abuse feel like no one understands them. Even if they have friends, family, and support, there is an internal emptiness.
- Problems with trust: After experiencing toxic relationships at work or in the family, it becomes hard for a person to trust even those who sincerely want to help.
- Emotional instability: One moment you may feel strong and confident, and the next — you could fall into an abyss of despair. Abuse makes your emotions chaotic and unpredictable.

Emotional abuse rarely stays only at the level of emotions and psyche. When a person lives in a state of stress, anxiety, and suppression for a long time, it inevitably starts to manifest physically.

HOW EMOTIONAL PAIN TURNS INTO PHYSICAL PAIN

The body reacts to emotional pain in the same way it reacts to physical pain: cortisol (the stress hormone) levels rise, the nervous system malfunctions, and internal organs start to suffer.

Physical pain, chronic illnesses, digestive problems, or sleep disorders — all of this can be a result of prolonged emotional pressure. Often, a person doesn't connect these symptoms with an abusive environment, but they are directly related.

Emotional abuse affects not only the psyche but also the body. Long-term stress causes the body to function in a constant state of tension, which can lead to:

- Sleep problems: Insomnia, nightmares, chronic fatigue.

- Stomach problems: Frequent stomach pain, digestive disorders (bulimia, anorexia, etc.).
- Headaches and body tension: Constant stress leads to muscle tightness, headaches, and back pain.
- Weakened immunity: A stressed body becomes vulnerable to viruses and illnesses.
- Appetite problems: Some people start overeating due to stress, others lose their appetite.

Let's look at how emotional abuse, experienced by our character-helper Sarah, not only destroyed her self-esteem but also reflected in her physical condition.

Sarah's Story

Sarah always believed in love. When she met Dan, he was caring, attentive, and told her she was special. She felt happy and protected. But over time, something changed. Dan began criticizing her over small things: first with subtle remarks — "Are you sure you want to wear that dress? It doesn't suit you," and then more harshly — "You're so clumsy, you can't do anything right." Sarah tried not to pay attention, thinking that he was just tired or going through a tough period.

But soon she noticed she no longer recognized herself. She started constantly doubting her actions, worrying about not irritating her partner. Her sleep became shallow and restless, waking up in the middle of the night with a sense of anxiety. During the day, she was plagued by headaches, and stress began to affect her stomach: first, mild discomfort, then regular pain and nausea.

Sarah began to lose interest in life. Dan often said that she couldn't do anything without him, and at some point, she believed him. She stopped meeting friends, was afraid to say anything "wrong," and therefore, kept silent and tried to avoid conflicts. But even that didn't help — Dan still found something to reproach her for. She started getting sick more often, felt constantly tired, but thought she was just not sleeping well. It wasn't until years later that she realized: her body was crying out for help, while she kept enduring.

Physical symptoms became a troubling signal that couldn't be ignored. She realized that emotional abuse doesn't just cause pain, it literally destroys her body.

HOW ABUSE AFFECTS SELF-ESTEEM

Emotional and physical abuse don't just cause pain in the moment — they slowly but surely destroy a person's self-esteem. At first, the victim resists, justifies themselves, but over time, constant criticism, humiliation, and manipulation become their inner voice. This doesn't happen in one day. It's a gradual process, like drops of water slowly eroding even the hardest stone.

When self-esteem collapses, a person stops seeing themselves as capable of change, loses confidence in their abilities, and stops trusting their own feelings. This leads to dependent relationships, constant approval-seeking, and an inability to set personal boundaries. It's important to recognize this process and understand that recovery is possible — but to do so, you need to start working on yourself and break free from the cycle of abuse.

Let's look at how this process manifests in the life of our second character, Emily.

Emily's Story

Emily always considered herself a confident person, but

after several years of living next to her toxic neighbor Mrs. Wright, her self-esteem began to falter. At first, she thought she was just being criticized for minor mistakes, but gradually she began to notice how her neighbor's words started echoing in her head.

Every time she did something in her apartment, she caught herself thinking, "What if Mrs. Wright will be unhappy again?" She began doubting her decisions, avoiding interaction with neighbors, feeling uncomfortable even in her own home.

1. Constant criticism becomes an inner voice. "You always make a mess!" "How can you be so irresponsible?" — Mrs. Wright repeated this over and over. At first, Emily was outraged, but then she began to think: "What if she's right? Maybe I really am doing something wrong?"

2. Comparing herself to others. "Look at the neighbor upstairs, her place is always tidy, and you can't even move the bike!" — Emily heard. She started believing she was worse than others, less organized, less worthy of respect.

3. Fear of making mistakes. Emily went out into the hallway less and less, tried to move more quietly, avoided conflicts. She was afraid that any action would trigger more criticism, and so she just tried to "keep a low profile."

4. Losing connection with herself. Emily once loved decorating her balcony, placing flowers by the door. But now, she was afraid it would provoke more comments and displeasure from Mrs. Wright. She began to wonder more and more: "What do I want? Or am I just trying to avoid criticism?"

5. Dependency on others' opinions. Emily became too dependent on her neighbor's mood. If Mrs. Wright was in a good mood, Emily felt relief. If she was cold and silent or made remarks — the day was ruined.

This process of self-esteem destruction happens not only in relationships with neighbors but also with family, at work, in friendships. When a person hears toxic words over and over, they begin to accept them as truth. But it's important to remember: these are not your thoughts, but other people's words implanted in your mind.

HOW TO BREAK OUT OF THIS CYCLE

Emotional abuse subtly infiltrates life, destroying the psyche, self-esteem, and even physical health. As the stories of Sarah and Emily show, abuse can manifest in different areas of life — at work, in the family, in relationships with a partner, or even with neighbors. But the most insidious part of it is its gradual nature. A person adapts, justifies others' behavior, and ignores the warning signs from their body.

But it's important to remember: this is not normal. This is not "difficulties that need to be endured." This is not "everyone goes through this." If you feel that something is wrong — then it is.

You don't have to tolerate toxic treatment. Your life and your health are more important than someone else's expectations, criticism, or manipulation. Recognizing the problem is the first step. And that means you are already on the path to change.

CAN YOU RECOVER?

Yes, but it's important to understand that while emotional abuse leaves deep scars, it is not a life sentence. A person can regain confidence, heal their mind, learn to trust again, and feel worthy of love and respect.

In the following chapters, we will discuss the first steps toward healing and recovery after emotional abuse.

CHAPTER 5
AM I EXPERIENCING EMOTIONAL ABUSE?

Abuse is not a loud argument that is immediately noticeable. It is a quiet poison that gradually seeps into life. Sometimes it hides behind care, sometimes behind jokes, sometimes behind "good intentions." But it's important to understand: if something inside you signals that "something is wrong," then most likely, it is. Let's explore how to recognize abuse and realize that it's time to take action.

I know that the topic of emotional abuse is heavy and painful. When we read about abuse, we don't always immediately recognize it in our own lives. Sometimes it seems like, "Well, everyone has problems," "He/She is just that kind of person," or "Maybe I'm overcomplicating things?"

Let's try to change the approach a little.

I suggest we relax and play a game of "True or False."

This will help you honestly look at your situation and figure out if abuse exists in your life — in relationships, in the family, at work, among friends.

The rules are simple:

Is this about me? — then it's worth thinking about. Mark a "+" in the box next to the question.

Is this definitely not about me? — great, move on and mark a "**-**" next to the question.

The main condition is honesty with yourself. Don't try to justify anyone or smooth things over. Just admit to yourself which moments resonate with your life.

Ready? Let's begin.

1. You Walk on Eggshells
True or False?

You're constantly thinking about how not to upset this person. You choose your words carefully, suppress your emotions, try to please, so there's no argument or cold silence. You feel like whether today will be a "good day" or a "bad day" depends on how you act and react.

● Does this apply to you? If yes, this is a warning sign.

2. Your Feelings Are a Joke
True or False?

You say, "I was hurt," and in response, you hear:

● "Oh, stop making things up,"
● "You're too sensitive,"
● "Stop dramatizing."

You're being told that how you feel doesn't matter, doesn't make sense, or is wrong.

If you recognize this in your life, think: why do your feelings not matter to someone?

3. You Apologize, Even When You're Not at Fault
True or False?

You notice that it's easier to say "sorry" than to explain or justify yourself.

You apologize even when you don't know for what — just to avoid conflict or "not ruin the mood" of the other person.
● You shouldn't have to constantly apologize just for existing.

4. Your Words Are Used Against You
True or False?

You shared something personal with someone, opened up about your feelings, and then heard it used against you as a reproach:
💬 "You said yourself that you're a failure,"
💬 "Of course, you're always scared."

Everything you once trusted is now being used against you.
✗ This is not care, it's manipulation.

5. You're Controlled, But It's Done "Out of Care"
True or False?

💬 "I just want what's best for you, so you shouldn't hang out with them."
💬 "I care about you, so I don't want you wearing that."
💬 "Do it my way — it's the right way."

A person dictates what you should wear, who you should be friends with, where you should go, and everything is presented as "care."

Care is about respecting your freedom, not limiting it.

6. You Lose Yourself
True or False?

You notice that you've stopped speaking, joking, laughing, being yourself around this person.

You're constantly tense, holding back, and thinking: "The most important thing is not to say something wrong."
● If you can't be yourself with someone, that's a dangerous sign.

7. Your Boundaries Are Disrespected
True or False?
You say:
💬 "I don't like this,"
💬 "I'm uncomfortable when you do this."
But in response, you hear:
💬 "You're just being picky,"
💬 "Stop being so sensitive,"
💬 "You're too touchy."
If your boundaries are mocked, this isn't love or friendship.

8. After Fights, They Become Affectionate, But It Repeats
True or False?
After an outburst of aggression, they apologize, say they love you, promise that "it won't happen again"...
But a few days later, everything repeats.
If you're stuck in this cycle, it's not a coincidence. It's a system

Results of the Game
- If you marked "+" on 2-3 points — it's worth thinking about.
- If "+" on 4-6 points — there are definitely elements of abuse in your life.
- If 7 or more — you're in an abusive relationship.

The main question: *Are you happy in this relationship?*
If your answer is "no," then it doesn't matter whether it meets the definition of abuse or not. You feel bad, and that's enough to make a change.
You have the right to comfort, respect, and freedom. No one can take that away from you.

WHAT TO DO NEXT? DON'T PANIC — THERE'S A WAY OUT
If after answering the questions you feel anxious or panic-ked,

that's normal. Realizing the problem is always a shock, but it's important to remember: you're not alone, and emotional abuse is not a life sentence. You can get out of this, recover, and build a life where you're respected.

A LITTLE ENCOURAGING STATISTICS

- 80% of people who realize they are in abusive relationships start looking for a way out. If you're reading this — you're already on the path to change.
- After leaving toxic relationships, people begin to notice improvements in their emotional state in just a few weeks.
- The more information a person gets about abuse, the faster they can get out of it. Awareness = strength.

You don't have to make any decisions right now or leave.

No need to panic — just keep reading. The more you understand, the clearer the steps will become to help you get out.

Abusive relationships are not forever. People get out of them and build happy lives.

Want Inspiration? Here Are Some Movies That Offer Hope:

- **Enough,** 2002 — a woman realizes her marriage is destroying her and finds the strength to leave.
- **Gaslight,** 1944/1947 — the classic story of gaslighting, where the main character realizes how she's being manipulated and frees herself.
- **Big Little Lies,** 2017-2019 — a series showing how women get out of abusive relationships, supporting each other.
- **The Wife,** 2017 — the story of a woman who has lived in the shadow of her husband but realizes her worth.

If you're scared — don't stop. Keep reading. The more you know, the stronger you become. You can change everything, and it's not as scary as it seems.

CHAPTER 6
THE DECISION: STAY OR LEAVE?

Having realized and accepted the fact that your relationship is far from healthy, many questions may arise in your mind: "What now? Should I leave right now? Maybe I'm exaggerating? Or should I try to change something?"

Don't panic right away. Not all abusive relationships are the same. In some cases, the situation indeed requires decisive action, but in others, it's possible to set boundaries, change the communication dynamics, and see if this leads to improvement.

Before making serious decisions, let's assess how critical your situation is and what options you have.

ASSESSING THE SITUATION: CRISIS OR SYSTEMIC ABUSE?

First, let's figure out what exactly you are facing: is it temporary difficulties or an established destructive pattern?

Here are signs that this is just a tough period, not abuse:

- Your relationship used to be healthy, but now you're facing challenges (financial issues, illness, stress).
- The person acknowledges their guilt and tries to change, instead of shifting the blame onto you.
- You can openly discuss your feelings, and after conflicts, there's real reconciliation, not just a temporary calm.

To better understand, let's consider Sarah's situation.

Sarah and her husband Dan were happy in their marriage, but in the last few months, he became irritable. He started having problems at work and often came home tired and silent. Sometimes, he would snap and be rude, but the next day he would apologize, explain that he didn't mean to hurt her, and try not to repeat his mistakes.

This is a crisis, not abuse. Dan isn't manipulating Sarah, he isn't devaluing her feelings, and he acknowledges his mistakes and works on them.

But it can be different. When unpleasant episodes become a system, and after bursts of "kindness" there's always another round of pain — this is emotional abuse.

WHEN TO RECOGNIZE THAT IT'S ABUSE? HERE ARE THE KEY SIGNS OF EMOTIONAL ABUSE:

- The person constantly causes you pain, not just during stressful moments.
- They blame you for their outbursts: "You drove me to this!"
- You feel overwhelmed, anxious, and constantly tense.
- After conflicts, they don't change their behavior but temporarily become "better" to avoid losing control over you.

Let's look at the example of our second heroine, Emily, and her boss, Mr. Peres.

Mr. Peres is sometimes friendly, may say something nice, or support an idea. But as soon as Emily relaxes, the situation repeats — he criticizes her, makes jokes at her expense in front of colleagues, forces her to work overtime without pay. If she tries to set boundaries, he responds: "You're too sensitive," "You just can't keep up."

This is already abuse. There's no respect, no effort to fix the situation, just a cycle of humiliation and "nice moments" to maintain control.

If you're struggling to understand where abuse ends and difficulties begin, ask yourself the key question:

If your friend or loved one were in your place, would you advise them to stay?

Your answer to this question can clarify a lot. When we look at other people's stories, we can see the truth more clearly than when we live inside the situation. Allow yourself to answer honestly.

DIFFERENT LEVELS OF ABUSE: YOUR SITUATION MAY BE DIFFERENT

All relationships involving abuse are different. Some people find themselves in an obviously dangerous situation and realize it, while others are just starting to wonder if something is wrong in their life. It's important not to compare yourself with others but to focus on your own situation. Let's consider three possible scenarios and understand what steps can be taken in each case.

1. You're Not Sure If This Is Abuse

You feel like something is wrong, but you're unsure whether it's really a problem or if you're exaggerating. You might justify the other person's behavior or blame yourself. In this case, don't rush into making decisions — first, you need to figure out the situation.

The first step — keep a journal of observations. Write down specific events, not just your emotions. This will help you see repeating patterns and understand how serious the situation is.

How to keep a journal?

Start a notebook, or create a document on your computer. The main thing is that no one else can read it. And as soon as something happens in your life that makes you feel down, make a note.

- Date it.
- Describe what happened (for example: "Today, he said I'm useless and that no one will ever love me").
- Write down how you felt at the time.
- Note how the person reacted if you indicated that you were uncomfortable.
- Analyze if this behavior repeats regularly.

If after a week or a month, reading your notes, you see that this toxic behavior repeated more than once — this is a warning sign.

The second step — setting boundaries. Often, abuse starts with small violations of personal space and comfort. Try to say clearly and calmly what you don't like.

IMPORTANT! This step is suitable when you can have some dialogue and the partner listens to you. But if you're in severe abusive relationships where you're scared and understand that the consequences of your words could be unpredictable, this step isn't for you.

For example: "When you say those things to me, it hurts. I don't want you to talk to me like that." If the person respects you, they'll at least try to change their behavior. If they keep ignoring your words, telling you that you're too sensitive or exaggerating, that's already a warning sign.

In the next chapter, we will go into more detail about how to set boundaries and what to do if the person ignores them.

2. You Realize That the Person Systematically Violates Your Boundaries, but You're Not Ready to Leave Yet

You realize that the situation is breaking you down, but you feel that you're not yet ready to take decisive action. Before making a final decision, it's important to understand what is keeping you in these relationships and how to protect yourself.

The first step — identify the factors preventing you from leaving. These could be:

- Fear that you won't manage without this person,
- Emotional attachment and hope that they will change,
- Financial dependence,
- Social pressure from family or friends,
- Fear of breaking up the family if there are children.

Understanding the reason will help you develop a strategy for leaving.

The second step — create a plan to protect yourself. If you're still in these relationships, you need to minimize the harm and protect yourself.

What can you do:

- Limit emotional contact, stop sharing your feelings with this person so they can't use them against you.
- Find support from others — a friend, therapist, support group.
- Prepare financially if there is dependence. Even small savings will help you feel more secure.

45

- Keep track of the moments of abuse in your journal to understand how the situation is developing and confirm that the problem is real.

Even if you can't leave right now, you can start protecting yourself right now.

3. You Feel That the Situation Is Dangerous, and the Cycle of Abuse Is Getting Worse

You realize that the relationship poses a threat not only to your psychological well-being but also to your physical safety. The person is becoming more aggressive, threatening, controlling you, and you see that things will only get worse.

The first step — don't tell the abuser your intentions. You can't say, "I'm going to leave you." You need to do everything quietly. If the person finds out that you're planning to leave, they may increase their control or threats.

The second step — prepare an exit plan.
What should you plan in advance:
- Where will you live after leaving? If possible, make arrangements with someone you trust.
- Which documents and items do you need to take with you? Gather them and keep them in a safe place.
- Do you have a financial cushion? Even a small amount for the first time is important.
- How to leave safely. It's best to do this when the abuser is busy or not at home.
- Who can you reach out to for support — friends, crisis centers, hotlines?

The third step — prepare a backup plan.
If you live with the abuser and the situation is becoming

dangerous, you need to think about how to leave urgently.

- Arrange with a friend or relative who can take you in case of danger.
- Find the contact information for crisis centers and hotlines in your area.
- Set up a "code word" with a close person, which will signal that you need urgent help.

If the situation is threatening, don't rely on the abuser's promises to change. Abuse doesn't disappear on its own.

WHAT YOU NEED TO REMEMBER

There's no universal solution for everyone. Some can leave immediately, while others need time and preparation.

You don't have to stay in relationships that cause you pain. If the situation worsens — leaving is necessary.

Safety always comes first. Even if you're not ready to leave yet, you can start protecting yourself now.

You're not alone in this situation. There's support, there are solutions, and you will definitely find your way out.

CHAPTER 7
FROM UNDERSTANDING TO ACTION

You've already passed an important stage: you've realized that emotional abuse exists in your life. Now you have a choice — stay and try to change the situation, or leave to protect yourself. We've already discussed that there is no universal solution, but in any case, you need to start working on yourself so that your life changes for the better.

Reading this book is already a step forward. You recognize the problem and are learning to spot the signs of abuse. But awareness is just the first part of the journey. To truly change something, you need to take action.

Imagine you're learning to swim. You could read dozens of books about swimming techniques, learn how to move your arms, how to breathe so you don't choke, but until you get in the water and try it yourself, you won't learn to swim.

The same goes for recovery. Without practice, new knowledge will just remain information. It won't change your internal state, help you regain your confidence, or teach you to set healthy boundaries.

That's why I didn't write just a theoretical book but also included a workbook. In the chapters of this book, there are practical exercises, but the workbook has even more. It is your personal tool for recovery after abuse, helping you:

- Recognize the feelings and beliefs left after emotional abuse.
- See hidden fears that prevent you from moving forward.
- Learn to defend your boundaries and protect yourself.
- Truly free yourself from the influence of the past.

You can complete the exercises alongside reading the book, gradually implementing changes in your life. This shouldn't be an additional burden — on the contrary, it's support that will help you recover and return to being your true self more quickly and easily.

You can already take a look at the practical part of the book and familiarize yourself with its content. But first, I want to draw your attention to a few important points when working with the workbook.

1. Don't rush. This is not a test that you need to pass, but a tool for your development.

2. Be honest with yourself. The "right" answer doesn't matter; what's important is your true feelings and thoughts.

3. If something is difficult — give yourself time. Some questions may bring resistance. That's normal. You can skip them for now and come back when you're ready.

4. Write as if it stays between you and the paper. This is your personal process. The more sincere you are, the more effective the work will be.

I'm sure you will figure everything out, and your recovery journey will be as comfortable as possible.

You've already taken the first step just by reading this book. Now, let's move forward.

CHAPTER 8
SETTING BOUNDARIES: HOW TO SAY "NO" AND STAND YOUR GROUND

If you've decided to stay in a relationship that seems toxic and hope to change it — that's okay. Not all life situations require an immediate breakup, especially if there isn't deep abuse. Relationships always involve friction, difficult periods, and misunderstandings, but the most important thing is not to stay silent about your feelings and needs. You need to communicate what you're comfortable with and what you're not.

If you want to try to shift the relationship from toxic to healthier, your main task is to learn how to set boundaries. This is a key step that will determine whether the dynamic of the relationship will change or stay the same. Without boundaries, any attempt to fix things will remain theoretical.

But what if you've already left — changed jobs, broken up with a partner, limited communication with relatives? Even then, boundaries are equally important. They will help you avoid falling into the same patterns, stop allowing people to violate your personal space, and, most importantly, help you get out of the victim role by learning to protect yourself.

This chapter will teach you how to set boundaries regardless of your situation. It's not about cold detachment or rigid control but about recognizing your worth and respecting yourself.

WHAT ARE BOUNDARIES AND WHY DO YOU NEED THEM?

Imagine you live in a house without a fence or doors. Anyone can walk in, take your food, use your things, and lie on your couch. You might get upset, but they will ignore you because you didn't set any boundaries and didn't make it clear what's acceptable and what's not.

Boundaries in life work the same way. If you don't define how people should treat you, they will decide that for you.

Boundaries are your personal fence, protecting your space, feelings, and comfort.

Boundaries help you understand what's comfortable for you and what's not.

Boundaries show others how to treat you.

Boundaries help eliminate anxiety and the feeling of being used.

Setting boundaries is not rudeness or selfishness; it's a way of saying to the world, "I matter too."

WHY ARE BOUNDARIES IMPORTANT FOR EVERYONE?

When it comes to abuse, many people immediately think of extreme situations where the victim is completely crushed and forced to run away. But in reality, boundary violations start long before the critical moment. They can be subtle, almost invisible, hidden behind jokes that hurt, covered by requests that are hard to refuse, and "wrapped" in words that leave you feeling guilty afterward.

- If you're in serious abusive relationships, boundaries will help you understand your value, realize that you don't deserve to be hurt, and start the process of escaping the situation.
- If you're dealing with lighter forms of abuse, boundaries will help prevent their escalation, boost your self-confidence, and help you avoid falling into a toxic cycle in the future.

We tend to think of boundaries as something sharp, rigid, or aggressive. But in reality, they're not about defending yourself from others; they're simply an important part of self-care.

Boundaries are not a way to defend yourself; they're a way to define what's acceptable to you and what's not.

I hope I've managed to show you that boundaries aren't a whim, but the foundation of healthy relationships.

Many people are afraid to set boundaries because they don't want to seem rude, selfish, or "inconvenient." Especially if they've spent a long time in an environment where their needs were ignored.

But I'll repeat:

◆ In healthy relationships, boundaries are the norm. They help two people understand each other better and respect each other's personal space.

◆ In toxic relationships, boundaries are a challenge. Someone who's used to controlling may resist, mock, or try to manipulate you.

Your life is your territory. No one can control your emotions or time unless you allow it.

Now let's look at examples of how boundaries were violated in the lives of Sarah and Emily.

Emily and the Toxic Friend

Emily has been friends with Anna for many years. Anna often borrows money from her but forgets to pay it back. She might also call her at 2 a.m. and say, "I'm feeling bad, you have to listen to me."

At first, Emily felt that this was how friendships should be — helping each other in everything. But then she noticed that this friendship wasn't bringing her joy, and she began to feel drained and increasingly used by Anna.

Now let's see what changes when Emily sets boundaries:

One day, Emily said, "Anna, I enjoy spending time with you, but it's important to me that you respect my boundaries. I can't answer your calls at night. Let's talk during the day instead."

Anna didn't like this and reacted angrily: "You've changed, you don't care about me anymore!"

Emily realized that this wasn't a real friendship, because healthy relationships aren't built on one-sided sacrifices.

It's important to understand: if someone truly values you, they will respect your boundaries. By trying to find a compromise, you will ensure that the communication is mutually enjoyable. But if your boundaries are ignored, the person won't listen to your words. Instead, they will start manipulating, blaming, and doing everything possible to regain control.

That's why boundaries aren't just a way to protect yourself; they're also an important indicator of whether you're being respected or used.

Sarah and the Manipulative Colleague

Sarah works in an office where her colleague Mark often shifts his work onto her. He says, "You're so fast, and I'm struggling, please help!"

Sarah didn't want to refuse but noticed that, due to this extra work, she didn't have time for her own tasks.

Now let's see what changes when Sarah sets boundaries:

She said, "Mark, I'm happy to help, but just this once. I can't do your work for you all the time."

How do you think Mark reacted?

Option 1: *He said, "Oh, sorry, I didn't realize I was overloading you."* — This is a healthy response.

Option 2: *He rolled his eyes and said, "What, are you too important? Why can't you help me? I'm struggling to finish everything on time!"* — This is manipulation.

Now You Understand Why Boundaries Are So Important? Boundaries are essential for understanding who you're dealing with.

HOW TO START SETTING BOUNDARIES

Now that you understand that boundaries are not rudeness, but self-care, let's break down how to set them.

Step 1: Identify what makes you uncomfortable.

If a conversation with someone leaves you feeling irritated, tired, or hurt, your boundaries are being violated.

Step 2: Formulate boundaries clearly (write down what should and shouldn't be said).

Bad example: *"You always interrupt me!"* — This is an accusation that will make the person defensive.

Healthy example: *"It's important for me to be heard. I don't like being interrupted."* — Here, you're expressing your feelings and needs, not accusing.

Step 3: Observe the reaction.

A person who respects you will listen and try to change their behavior for the sake of better communication.

A person who wants to control you will get upset, manipulate, or ignore your requests.

If someone continues to violate your boundaries, perhaps it's not about speaking more clearly, but rather reconsidering whether that person deserves your attention at all.

When you start setting boundaries, it might feel difficult at first. You may feel guilty or afraid that people will turn away because you're no longer as "accommodating."

But over time, you'll see that people who truly respect you will stay, while those who used you will leave on their own.

Boundaries are not about pushing others away; they're about surrounding yourself with the right people.

You don't have to immediately respond to messages if you don't want to or are busy. Sometimes, you need time to gather your thoughts, process information, or simply take a break from communication — and that's perfectly fine.

You can say "no" without long explanations. You don't need to justify yourself, look for valid reasons, or feel guilty just because someone might not like it.

You have the right to personal space and time for yourself. This is not selfishness, but self-care for your emotional state. If you need peace, to engage in your favorite activities, or simply rest, you don't have to sacrifice it for others.

And most importantly, you don't have to tolerate things that make you uncomfortable just because it's "expected" or "inconvenient to refuse." Respect for your boundaries starts with recognizing your own value.

LEARNING TO COUNTER VERBAL AGGRESSION

Words can wound just as much as actions. Sometimes verbal aggression is subtle, but over time, it chips away at your confidence and makes you doubt yourself. That's why it's important not only to recognize such situations but also to respond appropriately, protecting your boundaries.

Verbal aggression occurs when someone uses words to hurt, humiliate, or make another person feel bad. This can include yelling, insults, sarcasm, constant criticism, or even cold silence, which can be just as damaging as harsh words. Sometimes aggression is disguised: for example, someone says something hurtful but pretends it's a joke. The key is to recognize that if interactions with someone make you feel bad, anxious, or uncertain about yourself, it may not just be a conflict — it could be verbal abuse. And it needs to be confronted.

Let's explore ways to respond to such situations, ensuring you don't get drawn into conflict while still standing your ground.

Don't Justify Yourself. If you say, "I don't like this," and hear in response, "Oh, don't start," don't justify yourself. Simply repeat your stance: "I don't like this, and I won't tolerate it"—and don't tolerate it!

Don't Engage in Manipulation. If someone says, "You're too sensitive," you can respond with: "Maybe, but I still don't like it."

Set Clear Boundaries — And Be Ready to Enforce Them. If you say, "I won't allow you to talk to me this way" or "If you keep yelling, I will leave the room," you must follow through. Empty threats only reinforce the aggressor's belief that your words don't need to be taken seriously. If you're not prepared to act, it's better not to say it at all.

Evaluate the Behavior. If, after setting a boundary, the person continues to violate it, ask yourself: "Why should I tolerate this?" — and don't.

Below, I provide examples of how to protect yourself in different abusive situations. Everyone encounters moments where it's crucial to respond quickly and confidently to defend themselves and maintain inner peace.

1. How to Respond to Rudeness or Verbal Aggression

If someone starts speaking to you aggressively, try a simple but firm response:

☛ *"Stop talking to me like that!"* or *"Do not raise your voice at me!"*

Say it confidently and without hesitation. This response works in most situations and makes it clear that you will not tolerate verbal abuse.

2. How to Respond When Someone Ignores You

When a partner or acquaintance deliberately ignores you, this is often a form of manipulation or emotional neglect. If you find yourself in such a situation — whether at home, in a restaurant, or on vacation — and you're being ignored for a long time, don't suffer in silence. Instead, say directly: *"I'm bored being around you,"* and walk away.

Engage in something that makes you happy — read a book, meet friends, or take the kids to the park. The key is *not* to endure silent treatment or try to "melt the ice." Sometimes, unexpected behavior — like putting on headphones and singing along to a song — may provoke a reaction from your partner. And if it doesn't, at least you won't be sitting in misery.

3. How to Respond When Someone Constantly Contradicts You

If a colleague or partner constantly argues with everything you say—even when it's not a debate but just your opinion—you have every right to say:

☛ _"Stop!"_ or _"Enough!"_

Accompany this with a confident hand gesture, as if stopping traffic.

Then, calmly repeat your statement without further explanation. _Don't try to prove you're right_ — people who argue for the sake of arguing are not interested in dialogue; they just want to impose their opinions.

If someone tells you: _"You can't prove that!"_

Simply reply: _"No, I can't, but that's my opinion."_ — and immediately end the conversation.

Remember, _everyone has their own perspective,_ and if someone tries to convince you that your thoughts and feelings are "wrong," they are violating your boundaries. Instead of engaging in a pointless argument, _distance yourself_ — go for a walk, focus on your tasks, and don't let others control your mood.

The key takeaway: You have every right to your own opinions and feelings, and no one should make you doubt them.

4. How to Respond to Dismissiveness?

The first rule is don't explain or justify your emotions. Your feelings don't need approval! If someone tells you that you're overreacting or wrong about how you feel, stop them with a short phrase:

☛ _"Stop saying that!"_
☛ _"Don't tell me what I should feel."_
☛ _"Enough! I don't want to hear this!"_

A clear and firm response sets boundaries and shows that

you won't tolerate being dismissed.

If you're more surprised than angry by their behavior, try a different approach. Act as if you've had a sudden realization and say with genuine curiosity:

☛ *"Ah, so that's what you think!"*

This phrase is disarming—you're not justifying, defending, or agreeing. Instead, you're shifting the responsibility onto them.

5. How to Respond to Insults Disguised as Jokes?

Ever had someone say something rude, and when you objected, they smiled and said:

☛ *"Oh, come on, it's just a joke!"*

☛ *"You just don't understand humor."*

These statements are *not humor* — they are masked aggression. This can happen in families (when parents mock their children), at work (when a colleague makes sarcastic remarks), or among friends (when one person constantly jokes at another's expense but crosses the line).

The key takeaway: *When someone puts you down, they are trying to make themselves feel superior.*

When someone humiliates or mocks you, try calmly and confidently saying:

☛ *"Interesting... Did saying that make you feel powerful?"*

☛ *"Did that make you feel better?"*

These questions force them to think. Now, they must acknowledge that their comment was not "just a joke."

If they continue laughing or insist that you're "too serious," *don't explain why their joke was offensive* — you don't owe anyone an explanation. Simply disengage:

☛ *"I don't want to talk about this."*

☛ *"Let's discuss this later."*

Or better yet, just walk away. Someone who truly respects you will think about your words. Someone who uses humor as a weapon doesn't deserve your attention.

6. How to Respond to Blocking and Diversion

Have you ever asked someone a direct question, only for them to avoid answering, change the subject, or turn the conversation back on you? For example, you ask:

"Where did the $5,000 go?"

And instead of answering, they say:

"Oh, so now you're spying on me? Maybe I should give you a report on every step I take?"

This is called blocking and diversion — a tactic used to avoid answering a question by making you defend yourself instead.

How to handle it?

The key is not to fall for the provocation. If someone tries to steer the conversation away, don't explain, don't defend yourself, and don't argue. Just keep repeating your question.

☛ *"Look at me and answer: Where did the $5,000 go?"*

☛ *"Stop! I asked you a question. Answer it!"*

☛ *"Quit trying to distract me!"*

Repeat the question as many times as necessary. People who respect you will answer right away. Those who want to manipulate you will get irritated. But your goal is not to react to their emotions — it's to get a direct response.

Keep in mind that if someone persistently avoids answering, it's not accidental—it's intentional behavior. Your persistence is the best way to show that you won't be manipulated.

7. How to Respond to Accusations

Accusations are another form of verbal aggression. If someone constantly yells at you, calls you arrogant, stupid, dramatic, or accuses you of always wanting the last word, looking for trouble, or thinking you're smarter than everyone else, they are attacking you.

The mistake would be trying to explain that it's not true. Because by doing so, you give the aggressor exactly what they want — control over the conversation.

What to do instead?

Don't justify yourself or try to prove your innocence. Instead, stop the attack with firm phrases:

☛ *"Stop accusing me!"*
☛ *"Enough!"*
☛ *"I don't want to hear this again!"*

If the aggressor continues, remind them who they are talking to:

☛ *"Don't you dare speak to me like that!"*
☛ *"Remember who you're talking to!"*
☛ *"I don't think you really mean that."*

Important: Insulting words are not the truth — they are someone else's distorted version of reality. You don't have to believe them, and you certainly don't have to justify yourself.

Note: You should only use these responses if you are certain they won't provoke physical violence. In cases of severe abuse, setting boundaries in this way may not be effective and could even be dangerous.

8. How to Respond to Judgment and Criticism

Some people love to hand out negative judgments freely. They criticize your work, your abilities, and even your personality, acting as if they have the right to decide what kind of person you are.

But here's an important question: Who gave them that right?

"You're a terrible driver."

"You're too slow."

"You're acting stupid."

But you know what? Criticism and judgment are not the truth about you. They are simply opinions — often meant to diminish your self-worth.

How to respond?

Don't explain yourself. You don't have to prove that you can drive well or that you're not stupid. Instead, shut down the aggression with clear statements:

☞ *"Stop criticizing me!"*

☞ *"Quit judging me!"*

☞ *"Mind your own business!"*

☞ *"Keep your opinions to yourself."*

Then walk away from the conversation. Once you've set your boundary, don't engage any further — don't argue or defend yourself.

If the person truly meant to help, they will reflect on your reaction. But if their goal was simply to hurt you, you denied them that opportunity.

9. How to Respond When Someone Minimizes Your Achievements

Another form of verbal aggression is trivialization—when someone dismisses your efforts and makes it seem like your accomplishments are insignificant. The aggressor is trying to break down your confidence by convincing you that what matters to you isn't really important.

You say:

"I worked so hard on this!"

And they respond:

"Oh, big deal..."

This can happen at work, in families, or in relationships. It's as if the person is trying to make you believe that your efforts are meaningless.

How to respond?

☞ *"Hearing that doesn't feel supportive."*

☞ *"I wish you hadn't said that."*

☞ *"I've heard everything I needed to hear from you."*

Remember: You don't have to prove that your efforts matter. You know how much work you put in. Don't let others decide what's important for you.

Your feelings, achievements, and self-worth belong to you alone, and no one has the right to diminish them.

10. How to Respond to Disrespect

Disrespect is a subtle form of aggression. It can manifest as ignoring you, dismissing your words, mocking you, or acting as if your feelings don't matter.

But know this: No one has the right to treat you this way. If you feel disrespected, the best response is to speak up directly:

☞ *"I don't like how you're treating me!"*
☞ *"That was a low blow."*
☞ *"Stop this immediately!"*
☞ *"I have no interest in talking to you if you keep acting this way."*

11. How to Respond to Threats

Threats come in different forms. Sometimes they are direct:
"I'll hit you!" or *"You'll regret this!"*
Other times they are disguised:
"If you do that, I'll leave!"
"You know I can make your life miserable."
"Don't expect me to help you next time."

Remember, threats are manipulation. The person is trying to make you afraid so that you do what benefits them.

How to respond?

☞ *"Stop threatening me!"*
☞ *"I don't want to hear this!"*
☞ *"Leave me alone!"*

If you feel like a real threat is being made — seek help immediately. No one has the right to intimidate you, and you don't have to face it alone.

12. How to Respond to Name-Calling

Name-calling is a direct attack on your boundaries. It doesn't happen by accident — when someone calls you degrading names, they are deliberately trying to hurt you.

It doesn't matter why they do it — it's never acceptable. The best response is firm and outraged:

☛ *"Stop! Never call me that again!"*
☛ *"I don't allow anyone to speak to me like this!"*

If they continue, remove yourself from the conversation — or even better, from the relationship altogether.

It's hardest when the person insulting you is someone you love. But here's what you must understand: Love and respect go hand in hand. If someone doesn't respect you, they don't truly love you.

Many people who leave abusive relationships say they feel free afterward. And you, too, can choose freedom if someone refuses to respect your boundaries.

You don't have to tolerate abuse. You have the right to protect yourself and live in an atmosphere of respect.

13. How to Respond to Commands

You are an independent person. You have your own desires, your own decisions, and the right to be treated with respect. No one has the right to tell you what to do as if you were their subordinate.

However, sometimes people forget this and start giving orders:

"We're leaving!"
"Do this right now!"

"You have to!"

It's important to remember that if someone wants something from you, they should ask politely, not demand.

You can set boundaries by saying:

☛ *"Who exactly are you ordering around?"*
☛ *"Did you hear yourself?"*
☛ *"Could you ask nicely?"*
☛ *"I don't take orders!"*

If they use "we" to decide for both of you, like *"We're leaving,"* you can respond with:

☛ *"Well, I wasn't planning on going anywhere."*

A clear response sends the message that you are not a puppet and that your choices must be respected.

14. How to Respond to Denial and Gaslighting

You can't respond effectively to denial if you start believing the manipulator.

You express that something hurt you, made you uncomfortable, or upset you. But instead of acknowledging your feelings, they say:

"You misunderstood."
"I never said that."
"You're making things up!"

This isn't just denial — it's an attempt to make you doubt your own reality.

Some people do this deliberately to avoid responsibility. They insist that you misheard, misremembered, or misunderstood. And the more you try to explain or prove that you remember correctly, the deeper you fall into their trap. The more you argue, the more they deny.

So how do you respond to denial?

Don't justify yourself—shut it down immediately:

☞ *"Stop."*
☞ *"Don't distort the facts."*
☞ *"I trust my feelings and my memory."*

The most cunning form of denial is "forgetting." Keep in mind that when someone claims they "don't remember," they're often just trying to dodge responsibility.

You don't have to accept their supposed forgetfulness. You can say:

☞ *"I don't believe that. And I don't want this to happen again."*

Remember — if something hurt you, then it happened. No one has the right to dismiss your feelings or rewrite reality.

You don't need to prove you're right. You need to protect your boundaries.

Know this: every person is unique and deserves respect. No one has the right to hurt you, violate your personal boundaries, or make you feel like you're nothing.

CHAPTER 9
EMOTIONAL DIFFICULTIES WHEN MOVING FORWARD

This chapter is especially important for those who have already left an abusive relationship and are now trying to rebuild their life. The feeling of freedom can bring relief, but with it come complex emotions — fear, anger, guilt, and doubt. Sometimes, it seems that everything should get easier immediately after leaving, but in reality, the recovery process is a path that takes time and awareness.

However, even if you've decided to stay, this chapter is for you too. If your relationship can truly change with the proper boundaries in place, that's wonderful. But if, at some point, you realize that the situation is not changing and you still have to leave, it's important to know in advance what someone going through that process is experiencing. This will help you prepare, understand yourself, and recognize that any emotions during this period are part of the recovery process.

THE FIRST STAGE

When you finally decide to leave an abusive relationship, it feels like freedom, relief, and a new, better life are ahead. You think that you've left everything behind and can now just breathe deeply. But unexpectedly, you face emotions you weren't prepared for, because they overwhelm you in ways you didn't anticipate.

You expected ease, but instead, anxiety comes. You thought you'd feel joy, but instead, there's emptiness in your chest. You hoped for certainty in your decision, but doubts begin to torment you. Deep inside, there's a voice: "What if I made a mistake? What if I never meet a good person again? Maybe I exaggerated, and it wasn't that bad?"

This is disorienting. You left for a better life, so why is there so much chaos inside?

It's important to understand that these emotions are a normal part of the recovery process. You left behind a familiar world, even if it was painful. You stepped out of a system you had lived in for a long time, and now your mind is searching for new markers. This is why it's so important in the early stages of recovery to understand what you feel, identify where it's coming from, and figure out how to work with it. If you don't pay attention to these feelings, you could get stuck in them, doubting yourself, and even take a step back.

But why do these emotions come up when, seemingly, everything is behind you?

Because your psyche has finally relaxed. Imagine you've been carrying a heavy suitcase for a long time. While you carried it, you didn't have time to think — all your focus went into not dropping it and keeping yourself upright. But as soon as you set it down, you realize, "Wow... that was really heavy."

And in a moment, you feel the soreness in your arm — it's been holding that weight for too long. Your muscles were overworked, and now the pain will remind you of the tension you've been under all that time.

That's how emotions work. While you were in the abusive relationship, you lived in survival mode. You couldn't allow yourself to fully feel the pain — you had to cope, hold yourself together, adapt in the here and now. You couldn't relax for even a moment. And when you finally got out, your brain had the space to finally release everything you had been holding inside.

THE EMOTIONS YOU MIGHT FEEL
1. Emptiness

Sometimes, you don't feel pain or anger, just… nothing. It's as if there's a void inside. This is normal. For a long time, you invested your energy into a relationship that didn't give you back what you needed. Now, with everything over, that emptiness remains. This doesn't mean something is wrong with you. It's just a pause. A temporary calm before something new begins.

To better understand this, let's look at Sarah's situation.

After leaving a toxic relationship, Sarah thought the hardest part was behind her. No one controlled her, criticized her, or blamed her for everything. She could do whatever she wanted, talk to whoever she wanted, and go to bed when it was convenient, not when it was "right." This should have brought relief, but instead, she felt empty.

Every morning, she woke up with anxiety, although there were no more messages from Alex asking where she was, and then criticizing every word she said. For the first time in a long time, no one controlled her, but why did she feel so lost?

Walking past a café where they used to have breakfast, Sarah suddenly remembered how Alex would order her almond milk coffee because he knew she loved it. In that moment, it became hard for her to breathe. "Maybe he really cared about me? Maybe I was too demanding?" — flashed through her mind.

She knew Alex had caused her pain. She remembered feeling unnecessary, how he'd told her that she would never achieve anything without him, how she was afraid to say something "wrong." But now, with him no longer around, doubt consumed her. She didn't miss him; she missed the good moments, which were so few but had kept her in that relationship for years.

Sarah had thought that leaving an abusive relationship would lead to a new, free life, but it turned out that her emotions didn't let go so easily. She didn't expect it to be this hard at first.

2. Grief: Saying Goodbye Not Only to a Person but to a Dream

Sometimes, we think grief can only come from the death of someone. But grief isn't always about losing a person. It can also be about saying goodbye to your dreams, hopes, or things you longed for but never happened:

- The bitterness of a parent never being the way you needed them to be.
- The sadness of work relationships you built with hopes of a bright future, but they turned toxic.
- Disappointment in a friendship that only held together through your efforts.

Our heroine, Emily, also experienced these emotions after leaving her toxic relationship. Here's her story.

After leaving her job, Emily thought she would feel relief. There would be no more humiliation from her boss, no more constant tension and fear of his reactions. But instead of joy and freedom, she was overwhelmed by a sense of emptiness and disappointment.

She had invested so much in this job. When Emily first joined the company, she was full of enthusiasm. She thought she would build her dream career, that her ideas would be appreciated, and that management would see her as a promising specialist. She imagined growing into a leadership position, proud of her work.

But gradually, reality shattered her expectations. Instead of recognition, she received sarcastic comments; instead of support, constant reproaches. Her boss said she was "too slow," "too emotional," that her ideas "weren't good enough." Emily began doubting herself, but she kept trying — because maybe if she proved her worth, everything would change.

After leaving, she realized that she wasn't grieving the job itself, but the things she could have achieved there, given a healthy environment. She dreamed of colleagues who would respect her, of development, of work that would bring joy. But that dream never came true.

Emily had to accept that she didn't just leave a job. She said goodbye to the illusion she had held onto for so long. It was painful, but with that pain came the realization — now she had a chance to find a place where she would truly be valued.

But how do you cope with grief? After all, this is the very emotion that makes it impossible to move forward and enjoy life again. Here's what I suggest:

- Acknowledge it: "Yes, I am in pain." Don't come up with excuses. Just be honest with yourself: "I'm grieving not just because I lost a person, but also because I lost what I believed in."
- Write it down. Keep a journal. Write about what you miss, what's weighing on you. Sometimes, putting it all on paper makes it easier to bear.
- Give yourself time. There is no deadline for when it "should get better." Grief doesn't follow a calendar.

3. Anger

Anger is an emotion that often follows leaving toxic relationships. It may be directed at the abuser, at yourself, at circumstances, or even at people who didn't help when you needed support. And that's normal.

71

You might be angry at the person who caused you pain for years. You might be angry at yourself for not leaving sooner. You might be angry at friends and family who didn't notice the hell you were living in and didn't intervene or say, "Run."

Anger is not weakness, not a "bad" emotion, and not a sign that you're holding grudges. It's a natural response to injustice, pain, and suppression. If it didn't anger you how you were treated, that would be strange.

But what to do with this anger? You can't suppress it, but living in it constantly is not the solution either. Anger should become fuel for change, not a chain that keeps you stuck. It's needed to see the truth, recognize your worth, and never let anyone treat you the way they did before.

If you don't work through this emotion, it might get stuck inside. Instead of being freed, you'll keep returning to the past, to the grievances, to what you wish could have been changed but can't. It doesn't mean anger shouldn't exist. It means you should manage it in a way that helps you move forward, not drag you back into the past.

What to do with this emotion? How can you prevent it from destroying you and those around you? The key is to find healthy ways to release it — methods that allow you to free yourself from accumulated resentment without harming yourself or others. Let's explore how to process anger in a way that turns it into a tool for healing rather than a roadblock.

- Give it space. Close the door, grab a pillow, and... scream into it. Seriously. It helps.
- Write "anger letters." Not to send, but to pour out all the negativity onto paper. Write everything — anger, resentment, disappointment. Then you can tear up the letter or burn it (safely!).

- Move your body. Running, dancing, cleaning—physical activity helps "burn off" excess adrenaline and calm your anger.

The important thing is to figure out what works for you. When you feel angry, what brings relief? Maybe it's music, movement, physical activity, or talking to a friend. Find the methods that help you release emotions in a way that doesn't harm you or those around you.

4. Fear

Fear is an instinct given to us by nature — it helps us survive, warns us of danger, and teaches us caution. But when leaving an abusive relationship, this instinct often works against you. Even if the person who hurt you is no longer around, fear still holds you captive, keeping you on edge.

You may be afraid that you won't cope without them, that all that lies ahead is loneliness and disappointment. It may feel like the same thing will happen again — in new relationships, at a new job, with new people. This fear can make you doubt your choices, fear the unknown, and prevent you from moving forward.

Now it's time to learn how to tame your fear.

Most of the fear you experience is not based on reality. Instead, it feeds on worst-case scenarios created by your mind. The more power you give it, the louder it becomes. But when you start looking for evidence that contradicts your fear, its influence begins to weaken.

For example, if your fear tells you, *"You won't survive without them,"* stop and look at your life rationally. Haven't you already overcome difficult situations before? Haven't you solved problems, found ways out of tough situations? Maybe you've had to start over, change jobs, learn new skills, or go through painful breakups — and all of it made you stronger.

If your fear whispers, *"You'll never meet a good person,"* ask yourself, *"What is this thought based on?"* Are there not happy relationships around you? Haven't you met kind and caring people before? If they exist, then the possibility of building a healthy relationship is real.

Fear will try to convince you that you are powerless, that the future is scary and uncertain. But if you start looking for facts that prove otherwise, you will see that your opportunities are much greater than your fear suggests. The more proof you find that you are capable of handling challenges, the weaker your fear will become.

A Simple Exercise to Overcome Fear

Take a piece of paper and a pencil, and write down your fear. Name it.

Not just *"I'm scared,"* but: *"I'm afraid of being alone. I'm afraid of trusting again."*

When fear has a name, it loses some of its power.

Then ask yourself: *"What will happen if my fear comes true?"*

The answer often surprises people.

For example, an internal dialogue might go like this:

"I'm afraid of being alone."

"And what will happen if I end up alone?"

"I'll feel sad."

"And?"

"But I've dealt with sadness before."

Talking to your fear isn't about fighting it — it's about understanding it. You don't have to believe everything fear tells you. You can listen, analyze, ask questions, and find proof that it's wrong. And in that moment, you stop being afraid.

5. Guilt and Doubt: The Uninvited Guests That Won't Leave

Guilt and doubt are some of the hardest emotions because

they make you question yourself. They sneak into your mind like uninvited guests, appearing out of nowhere and refusing to leave.

You might suddenly think: *"Was I too harsh when I set boundaries with my mother?"* or *"Maybe I should have tried one more time to fix things with my ex?"*

And sometimes the thought is even more painful: *"What if it was my fault? Maybe I deserved the way my boss treated me?"*

But the truth is — you are not responsible for someone else's harmful actions. You are not to blame for the pain someone else caused you. You were not obligated to endure and wait for them to change.

And yet, even understanding this logically, guilt can still creep in, replaying the past in your mind, making you wonder if you should have acted differently. In these moments, it's important to separate facts from emotions.

Your emotions might whisper, *"I let this person down."*

But if you look at the situation clearly, the truth might be: *"I tried to express my needs, but they didn't listen."*

One of the best ways to deal with guilt is to imagine a close friend going through the same thing.

If a friend said, *"I feel guilty for ending a toxic relationship,"* what would you tell them? Most likely, you'd reassure them that they made the right choice, that they deserve better.

So why can't you say the same to yourself?

Sometimes, to let go of the past, all you need is a shift in perspective.

- Instead of *"I failed,"* tell yourself: *"I did my best, and I chose myself."*
- Instead of *"I ruined this relationship,"* say: *"I put myself first."*

This isn't self-deception — it's simply another way of seeing reality. One that gives you strength instead of taking it away.

Guilt and doubt often resurface unexpectedly, even when nothing triggers them. The day might be going fine, the past seems far behind, and suddenly — anxiety, tears, or even anger appear. That's normal.

Emotions don't disappear overnight — they come in waves.

WHY DO EMOTIONS FEEL LIKE WAVES?

Because they come and go. They don't stay forever.

One moment, you're sitting, drinking tea, feeling fine—and suddenly, it hits you. Sadness. Or anger. Or anxiety. Like a wave.

And you know what's important? Every wave recedes.

It rises, peaks, crashes over you... and then fades away. Always.

Sometimes it feels like you're drowning in it. But you're not. The fact that you're reading this now means you're already staying afloat.

Understanding that emotions come and go is the first step. But what do you do when the wave crashes over you, when the pain or anxiety feels too strong?

What not to do? Don't suppress your emotions.

Trying to suppress emotions is like trying to hold a beach ball underwater—the deeper you push it down, the stronger it bursts back up.

Repressed feelings don't disappear. They accumulate inside, turning into chronic stress, anxiety, exhaustion, or even physical illness. Instead of fading away, they find other ways to manifest — making the pain even deeper and harder to handle.

So What Should You Do?
- If you feel like crying — cry. Tears are a natural way to release pain.

- If you feel angry — find a safe way to let it out. Scream into a pillow, shout in your car, or even go on a roller coaster where no one will judge you.
- If you feel anxious — move your body. Take a brisk walk, go for a run, dance to loud music. Movement helps discharge emotional tension.

The key is to acknowledge your emotions.

Don't run from them. Strength isn't about feeling nothing—it's about recognizing and accepting your emotions, and still moving forward.

And in moments of despair, remind yourself: this will pass.

You've survived pain before, and you're surviving it now. You are stronger than you think.

CHAPTER 10
RESTORING YOUR SELF-ESTEEM

The path to recovery is not a quick one, but a sequential process. Today, we move on to the next stage: restoring your self-esteem.

Self-esteem is the foundation upon which your confidence, decisions, and relationships with the world are built. It shapes how you perceive yourself, what kind of relationships you choose, and how much you value yourself in work and life. Abusive relationships — whether in the family, at work, in friendships, or with a partner — inevitably destroy this foundation. Constant criticism, manipulation, and devaluation erode inner self-confidence, leaving behind doubts and anxiety.

But the good news is that self-esteem can be restored. Whether you're in the process of leaving toxic relationships or trying to improve existing ones, working on your self-esteem is beneficial for everyone. It will help you set healthy boundaries, stop doubting your worth, and make decisions based not on fear, but on self-respect.

Let's explore how to begin this journey and how to step by step regain your confidence.

Self-esteem is not just what you think about yourself. It's also how you feel when you look in the mirror. It's the inner voice that quietly and confidently says:

"You can do this."
"You deserve love and respect."
"Your feelings matter."

This voice has lived inside each of us since childhood. It is formed from how we were supported, how we were spoken to, and how others reacted to our successes and mistakes. But when you've been in toxic relationships for a long time, this voice becomes quieter. It's drowned out by other voices. You may be wondering whose voices could be so powerful that they drowned out your own? They might be:

- The voice of your partner, who constantly criticizes and devalues: *"Without me, you're nothing," "You can't do this right."*
- Or the voice of a controlling parent, who instills: *"You're not good enough," "You need to try harder to earn my love."*
- Or the voice of a boss, who says: *"You're not managing," "You're useless without me."*
- Or maybe the voice of a "friend," who teases and makes "harmless" remarks: *"You're so naïve," "You never think things through."*

Over time, you stop noticing that these words aren't yours. They become background noise. Like the radio playing in the background — you don't actively listen to it, but it still affects your mood and your opinion of yourself.

To better understand how this works, let's look at the stories of Sarah and Emily.

Sarah's Story: When Others' Expectations Become Your Own

Sarah worked for a large company. She was a responsible and diligent employee, always ready to take on a task, stay late, and help a colleague. But she had a boss who was never satisfied with her work.

Every time Sarah submitted a project, he found something to criticize:

"You did it wrong again, not how I asked."

"This is basic stuff, why didn't you figure it out?"

"Without my help, you wouldn't have managed at all."

At first, Sarah thought, "He's just strict, I need to try harder." She stayed late, double-checked every detail, trying to anticipate his expectations. But no matter how hard she worked, her boss always found something to criticize.

Over time, Sarah began to believe she was truly "incompetent" and couldn't do her work without mistakes. Even when colleagues praised her, she thought, "They just don't know the real me." Her inner confidence disappeared. She was afraid to speak up in meetings, thinking her suggestions would be mocked. And she started doubting all her future decisions.

The paradox was that Sarah was an excellent professional. It was just that her boss's voice had become so loud in her head that it drowned out her own voice.

Emily's Story: Toxic Friendship Under the Guise of Care

Emily had been friends with Anna since college. They were always there for each other: sharing secrets, spending weekends together, discussing their relationships. But over time, something started to change.

Anna often made "joking" comments:

"Why are you so naïve? Everyone can see that he's not right for you."

"Did you really choose that dress? Seriously? It makes you look bigger."

"You're overreacting. Relax already."

At first, Emily didn't pay much attention. She thought, "Well, it's just Anna. She's just honest. That's just how she communicates."

80

But over time, she started doubting herself. When she was getting ready for a meeting, she thought, "What will Anna say about this outfit?" When making decisions, she asked herself, "Would Anna do this?" She became afraid of doing something "wrong" to avoid hearing sarcastic comments.

Emily didn't even notice how she gradually stopped trusting herself. She got used to thinking her decisions were "wrong," her feelings were "too dramatic," and her taste was "questionable."

Do you see the point? Anna never yelled at Emily. She didn't openly humiliate her. But her "friendly advice" slowly eroded Emily's self-esteem, just like water slowly wears down stone.

Both Sarah and Emily faced different forms of emotional abuse.

For Sarah, it was direct criticism and devaluation at work.

For Emily, it was subtle manipulation in a friendship, disguised as "care."

But the result was the same: they started to believe that something was wrong with them.

WHY ARE WE SO VULNERABLE TO THE INFLUENCE OF OTHERS' OPINIONS?

Because our brain tends to believe repetitive information. If you hear often enough, "You can't do anything" or "What you do is never enough," at some point your brain stops challenging it and starts accepting it as fact. Even if inside you, something whispers, "This isn't true," the abuser's voice becomes louder.

But here's what's important to remember: You weren't born with this voice in your head. It appeared because someone, at some point, repeatedly told you that you weren't good enough. And if that voice was imposed, it means it can be replaced.

Now that we've explored how abuse affects self-esteem, let's move on to how to regain your inner voice. The one that says:

"You are worthy."

"You are strong."

"You matter."

Below, I'll list some exercises that can help restore your self-confidence, but you need to practice them several times.

1. Exercise: "I Am More Than..."

When someone repeatedly tells you that you're "not this," you begin to believe it. It's time to take back your "I."

Take a piece of paper and write:

"I am not just my mistakes. I am my experience, my efforts, my strength."

"I am not just someone's daughter, wife, or employee. I am me."

Emily tried this exercise and wrote:

"I am not 'too sensitive.' I am attentive and compassionate. This is my strength, not a weakness."

2. Exercise: "My Strengths"

Make a list of your positive qualities. Don't be afraid to write even the simplest ones:

"I am a good listener."

"I cook well."

"I love animals."

These may seem like small things, but they are you. Your value isn't just measured by big achievements.

At first, Sarah couldn't think of anything. But as she started writing, she remembered how she helped a colleague with a project, how she supported a friend in tough times, and how she learned to cook her favorite dish. She suddenly realized: *"I'm not 'worthless,' I just forgot how much I can do."*

3. Exercise: "The Mirror of Truth"

Look at yourself in the mirror and say aloud:

"I deserve respect."

"My feelings matter."

"I don't have to be perfect to deserve love."

This may feel strange or awkward at first. But try it. The voice you speak aloud is louder than the inner critic.

It may be difficult at first. You might even shed some tears. That's normal. Keep going. You are remembering how to love yourself.

4. Exercise: "I Can Do It"

In her book Stopping Wife Abuse, Jennifer Baker Fleming lists statements that help victims gather their strength and think better of themselves. I've modified and added some here. Read them and feel them.

"I can trust my feelings and impressions."

"I am not responsible for someone else's irritation, anger, or rage."

"I deserve freedom from emotional pain."

"I can say 'no' when I don't like something or don't want it."

"I am an important person."

"I am a valuable person."

"I deserve to be treated with respect."

"I have power over my own life."

"I can take care of myself."

"I can decide what's best for me."

"I can change my life if I want to."

"I am not alone; I can reach out to others for help."

"I am worthy of people working on themselves and changing for me."

"I deserve a safe and happy life."

"I can rely on my resourcefulness and ingenuity."

It's never too late to start rebuilding your self-confidence. This will be a challenging path, but you will succeed. And during those moments when you feel like giving up, and the voice of the abuser in your head tries to regain control over your thoughts, return to this chapter or open the workbook at the end of the book and do any self-esteem exercise.

Day by day, you will begin to appreciate and love yourself more. And in time, the foreign voice with its negative beliefs will permanently leave your mind and heart.

CHAPTER 11
FINDING YOURSELF AFTER ABUSIVE RELATIONSHIPS

When you've been in toxic relationships for a long time, your boundaries begin to blur. You get used to not focusing on your own desires, but instead, on the needs of others. Perhaps you were told that your dreams were foolish, that your feelings didn't matter, and that your worth depended on how well you met someone else's expectations. You might have adapted to avoid conflict, pleased others to avoid rejection, and forgotten your real needs because they held no weight in the eyes of the abuser.

But now everything has changed. Now, you are free. But what does that mean?

Some people, after leaving toxic relationships, think: "Now I will start living!" — but they face the dilemma of what to do next. Years of suppression and constant tension leave their mark. You might have gotten used to being directed, evaluated, and corrected, meaning others made all the decisions for you. Now, when there's no one dictating how to live, you realize you don't know what you actually want. And that's normal.

But what will happen if you leave everything as it is? If you simply go with the flow, not asking yourself questions, not exploring who you are? On the surface, everything might seem fine. You work, take care of things, meet people. But deep inside, you feel like you're not living, just existing. You might find yourself back in relationships where your boundaries are violated — not because you want it, but because you don't fully understand what kind of relationship you really need. You may continue making decisions based on others' expectations rather than your true desires. And a few years later, you might again ask yourself, *"Why do I feel unhappy if everything seems fine?"*

If you choose the path of self-awareness, your life will begin to fill with meaning. You will start to see the difference between what truly matters to you and what was imposed upon you. You will understand which people bring you joy and which ones drain your energy. You will learn to make choices consciously, not out of fear or habit. It's not a quick process, but every step along the way will bring you closer to your true self.

Remembering who you are means reclaiming the right to be who you are. You've always had this right, even if someone once convinced you that you didn't deserve it. But that's not true. You have every right to be yourself. And now is the time to begin this journey.

STEP 1: RECLAIM THE RIGHT TO WANT

Have you ever felt like your life was on autopilot? Like you wake up, go through the motions, but don't feel any true desire to do anything? You might watch a movie someone recommended, cook a meal that someone else liked, or go to a job that seems logical... but you don't feel yourself in it, you don't get any joy from it.

When you constantly put someone else's needs above your own, you gradually stop listening to your own desires. And if you've been told things like: *"You always want something silly,"* *"That's not serious," "That won't do you any good,"* it's natural that your desires simply fade away. But here's the question: where do they go?

The answer is simple: they don't disappear. They hide under layers of fear, uncertainty, and the habit of adapting to others' expectations. Reclaiming your right to want means allowing yourself to ask questions. What do I love? What brings me joy? What gives my life meaning? If you find it hard to answer these questions right now, try a small exercise.

The "Memory Box" Method

Take a piece of paper or open your phone's notes. Try to remember moments in your life when you truly felt happy. Not just "okay," but when happiness really filled you up.

Think back to your childhood. What excited you? Did you love to draw, play with building blocks, read, dance? When did you lose track of time because you were fully immersed in an activity?

Think about your youth. What were your dreams? What did you fantasize about when no one judged you? Maybe you wanted to travel, engage in creative activities, or try something new?

Think about recent moments of joy. What brought you pleasure, but you postponed it for various reasons? Perhaps it was solitary walks, reading certain books, doing sports, or spending time with friends without rushing?

Write down these moments. The more details, the better. What time of year was it? What sounds, smells, and sensations surrounded you? These are not just memories — they are keys to understanding yourself.

What if I can't remember anything?

Sometimes, desires are so deeply hidden that it's hard to find them right away. That's okay. Try another approach: observe your reactions in everyday life.

What topics spark your interest, even if you don't realize why?

What do you read or watch videos about when you have free time?

What kind of people do you admire?

Sometimes our desires show themselves indirectly, through subconscious reactions. For example, you might feel inspired by stories about travelers or people who started their own businesses. Or you might be drawn to tales about psychology, art, or sports.

Record your observations. Even if there's no clear answer yet, the process of searching is already progress.

Important: Don't Pressure Yourself

You don't have to immediately find your path. This is not a test where you need to give the "right" answer. It's self-exploration, and it may take some time.

Allow yourself to try new things, even if you're unsure whether you'll like them. Sign up for dance lessons, start learning a foreign language, try drawing, cook a new dish every week, or simply walk around unfamiliar places. Give yourself the freedom to experiment and play without the fear of making a mistake.

The more you try, the clearer it will become what you truly want.

STEP 2: LEARNING TO TRUST YOURSELF

Self-trust is the foundation on which your entire life is built. You trust your own taste when choosing food or clothing. You trust your intuition and reasoning when making important decisions. You trust your emotions when you sense that something is wrong. That's natural.

But sometimes this mechanism fails. At some point, you begin to doubt your own desires and intuition. You wait for external approval, fear making the "wrong" choice, and feel anxious about even the simplest decisions. You develop a habit of wanting someone else to take responsibility, believing that they surely know better how life should be lived.

Why does this happen?

Because someone or something made you believe that you are incompetent. As a result, you lose confidence in yourself and start seeking validation from others. Or you wait for someone to tell you what to do next.

Some people are confident in themselves and their choices. They know what they want and aren't afraid to express it. They're not scared of making decisions because they understand: even if things don't go as planned, they'll handle it. They are open to new opportunities, unafraid of change, and see mistakes not as catastrophes but as lessons to learn from.

Then there are those who constantly doubt themselves. They are afraid to make decisions without external approval, postpone important steps for fear of failure, and often miss great opportunities. Instead of following their own desires, they adjust to others' expectations just to avoid judgment. Any change triggers anxiety because an inner voice whispers: "You won't be able to handle it" or "Are you sure you're doing the right thing?"

What's the difference between someone who trusts themselves and someone who doesn't?

A self-confident person takes responsibility for their own life.

They don't wait for someone to tell them what to do. They trust their feelings, desires, and decisions. They know how to say "no" when something doesn't suit them, and they clearly understand what they want from life.

That is true freedom.

Feeling confident and taking control of your own life is not an inborn gift — it's a skill. And the good news is that it can be learned. Right now, you may feel like you've lost trust in yourself, like you don't know what you want or are afraid of making the wrong move.

But the truth is, you have always been in charge of your own life — even in moments when you didn't realize it. You've made decisions, overcome difficulties, and found ways out of tough situations.

Now it's time to reclaim that ability. You can learn to listen to yourself again, to make choices without fear, and to move forward without hiding from life. Because if you keep doubting and retreating like a turtle into its shell, you risk missing out on so much that life has to offer.

And don't be afraid to make mistakes — because mistakes are normal, and failures are just part of the journey. The most important thing is not to let fear paralyze you. You've already taken a huge step toward regaining control over your life. Now let's figure out how to rebuild self-trust.

Here are a few highly effective exercises. They are simple but will significantly strengthen your ability to trust yourself.

The Practice of Small Choices

To regain confidence in your ability to make decisions, start with the simplest ones.

Every day, ask yourself questions like:

✓ *What do I want for breakfast today?*

✓ *What music do I feel like listening to?*
✓ *What clothes feel comfortable right now?*
✓ *What do I want to do this evening?*

When you make conscious choices, you strengthen your connection with yourself. You get used to the idea that your desires matter, and over time, you stop second-guessing every action.

The Elimination Method: "What Do I Definitely Not Want?"

Sometimes, it's harder to figure out what you do want than to recognize what you don't want. Try approaching it from the opposite direction. For example:

✗ *I don't want to work in a noisy office.*
✗ *I don't like running in the mornings.*
✗ *I don't enjoy being in groups where I feel out of place.*

Now, turn these "don'ts" into "dos":

◼ *I enjoy working in a quiet environment.*
◼ *I love slow walks in the park.*
◼ *I feel comfortable with people who understand me.*
Gradually, you'll define your true desires.

Self-Observation Journal

To restore your connection with yourself, start writing down moments when you felt joy, comfort, or confidence.

Every evening, jot down at least one thing that brought you pleasure during the day.

For example:

- *"Today, I picked a movie myself, and I really enjoyed it."*
- *"I declined an invitation that didn't interest me, and I felt relieved."*
- *"I cooked a meal I love and enjoyed the process."*

At the end of the week, reread your notes. You'll start to see patterns — what truly brings you joy and what genuinely matters to you.

Self-trust is not an instant switch — it's a process. You can't regain confidence overnight. But every time you make a choice that honors yourself — even a small one — you strengthen that trust.

You already know what you need. You just have to give yourself permission to feel it again.

STEP 3: STOP LIVING BY OTHER PEOPLE'S RULES

In the chapter on self-esteem, we discussed how if you hear the same thing repeatedly, you eventually start believing it. This is how false beliefs, shaped by toxic environments, take root.

If someone kept telling you:
- *"You'll never achieve anything."*
- *"Your desires don't matter."*
- *"You're not good enough."*

Then over time, these words become your inner reality.

But the truth is, these are just baseless statements — you can challenge them and replace them with more positive beliefs.

Exercise: Rewriting Beliefs

Take a sheet of paper and divide it into two columns.

In the first column, write down all the negative beliefs you've absorbed from toxic relationships.

For example:

✗ *"I'm useless."*

✗ *"I'm too weak to change anything."*

✗ *"I'll never succeed."*

Now, in the second column, rewrite them into new, supportive beliefs:

■ *"The people who truly matter appreciate me."*
■ *"I've already started changing, which proves my strength."*
■ *"I have a chance at success if I try."*

Read the second column out loud. At first, these words may feel unfamiliar, but over time, they will become a part of you and inspire you to take action.

STEP 4: FIND YOUR PLACE IN LIFE — THROUGH ACTION, NOT WAITING

After completing the first three steps — learning to understand your desires, trust yourself, and let go of limiting beliefs — you'll face the most important question: What's next? It's normal to feel a sense of emptiness after leaving a toxic relationship. When someone else has been dictating how you live, what you feel, and what decisions to make for a long time, the absence of that control can feel overwhelming. But this state is not a loss — it's an opportunity to fill your life with what truly matters to you.

1. Identify What Makes You Feel Alive

For a week, write down two things every day:

✓ *What gave me energy today?* (A conversation with a friend? A walk? A favorite book? A creative hobby?)

✓ *What drained my energy?* (What made me feel exhausted, irritated, or like my day was wasted?)

At the end of the week, review your notes. You'll start to see patterns — what you should do more of and what you need to eliminate.

2. Find People Who Support You

Surrounding yourself with the right people plays a huge role

in self-discovery.
- Join a club or community that interests you.
- Find like-minded people online.
- Identify which people in your life uplift you and which ones drag you down.

Your place in life won't find you — you have to find it.

You don't need to have all the answers right away. Keep exploring, experimenting, and moving forward — because you have the right to build a life that feels right for you.

CHAPTER 12
REALIZING YOUR STRENGTH AND INDEPENDENCE

The fear of loneliness and self-doubt does not only manifest after leaving toxic romantic relationships. This fear can arise after leaving a destructive family, changing jobs, breaking off a friendship, or even when someone stops interacting with manipulative relatives.

Imagine someone who has lived in a family for a long time where they were constantly criticized: "You'll never achieve anything without us," "You can't manage," "You don't know how to make the right decisions." Or an employee who worked under the pressure of a toxic boss, accustomed to constant control, and now, after leaving, doesn't know how to act independently.

When someone stops fearing loneliness, they don't feel emptiness, but space. Space for self-discovery, for joy, for peace. You begin to understand that you don't need someone else to feel complete. This doesn't mean you're doomed to be alone. It means you're learning to be happy both alone and in relationships because now your value doesn't depend on someone else's presence.

To begin with, you need to stop fearing loneliness and learn to be a self-sufficient person. Self-sufficiency is not just the ability to be alone; it's the ability to build your life without the fear of silence and without constantly seeking external approval. It's a skill that changes everything: how you work, how you choose friends, how you build relationships.

You're already on this path. You're learning to recognize your desires, defend your boundaries, and build a life where you are not suppressed but respected. It's a process, but it starts with realizing: your value doesn't depend on others. You're not someone's appendage, not a shadow, not an easy version of someone else. You are a full person.

Here are some recommendations on how to stop fearing loneliness:

1. Stop Viewing Loneliness as a Deficiency

Often, the fear of loneliness is linked to negative beliefs: "If I'm alone, there's something wrong with me," or "No one needs me." In reality, loneliness is just a state that can be used for your benefit. Try changing your perception: instead of "I'm alone," think "I'm free." This is time you can dedicate to yourself: growing, learning something new, resting the way you want.

2. Develop Independence in Everyday Life

Simple everyday things help build confidence in yourself. For example:

- Learn to spend time alone: go to a café, take a walk, or go on a mini-trip.
- Develop skills that make you more independent: cooking, financial literacy, organizing daily life.
- Learn to make decisions without looking for others' approval. Start small: choose a movie without advice, decide how you'll spend the weekend based on your own desires.

3. Identify What Energizes You

Self-sufficient people aren't afraid of being alone because they know how to fill that space. Find activities that bring you joy and passion. These could be new hobbies, sports, learning languages, or creative pursuits. It's important that these activities bring you joy for yourself, not because they're "trendy" or "correct."

4. Work on Your Inner Dialogue

Someone who fears loneliness often criticizes themselves and waits for external validation of their worth. Start observing your thoughts: if you notice self-criticism, ask yourself, "Is this true? Or is it just fear talking?" Gradually, change your inner voice to one that is more supportive.

5. Don't Fill the Void with People Who Aren't Necessary

Sometimes, the fear of loneliness drives us to hold on to toxic relationships, even if they're destroying us. It's important to learn to be alone without feeling lonely. Before starting new relationships or friendships, ask yourself: "Do I feel good with this person? Or am I just afraid to be alone?"

6. Create Your Support System

Being self-sufficient doesn't mean being alone. It just means your value doesn't depend on other people. But it's important to surround yourself with those who support you: friends, mentors, like-minded individuals. Learn to consciously choose your environment — let it be filled with people who respect you and inspire you.

7. Record Your Achievements

Every day, mark small victories: "Today, I spent the evening peacefully without anxiety," "I made a decision on my own," "I didn't seek approval from others. " This will help you see that you are truly moving forward and becoming more self-sufficient. Self-sufficiency is not about loneliness, it's about freedom. When you stop fearing being with yourself, life becomes simpler, calmer, and more interesting.

HOW TO LEARN TO RELY ON YOURSELF IN ANY SITUATION

You are much stronger than you think. Inside you is an incredible resource that may have been suppressed for years by abuse, criticism, and doubts. You might have been made to believe that you're weak, that without someone else, you couldn't manage, that your decisions were wrong. But the truth is, you've already proven that you can handle things. Since you're reading this book and walking the path to recovery, you already have inner strength. It's just time to acknowledge it and develop it.

Relying on yourself doesn't mean doing everything alone. It doesn't mean you'll never ask for help. It means that even if help doesn't come, you will find a way. It's not about the absence of fear, but about the ability to move forward despite it. It's the understanding that you're capable of making decisions and being confident in them, that you can handle life's challenges by relying on your own resources.

Relying on yourself means that even if help doesn't come, you will find a way out on your own.

When a person begins to rely on themselves, they stop being a prisoner of others' opinions and circumstances. They no longer wait for external approval, are not afraid to try new things, and don't see mistakes as catastrophes. They embrace their strength and understand that their value doesn't depend on others' recognition. This is freedom.

But how to achieve this?

It's a process that takes time, but every step on this path makes you stronger. Here are some ways to start:

1. Notice Moments When You've Already Managed

We often underestimate our successes, especially if we've had someone who made us feel like we couldn't do anything. So do this exercise.

Practical Exercise: Create a list of victories. Write down everything you managed to accomplish, even if it seems like a small thing.

For example: *"Today I said no," "I expressed my opinion," "I made a decision on my own."*

The more entries you make, the clearer it will become: you are already handling things.

2. Stop Seeking Approval from Others

If you care about others' opinions, that's okay. But if you can't make a decision without confirmation from others — that's a sign that you're giving your life into someone else's hands.

What to do?

When you catch yourself wanting to ask for an opinion, first answer that question yourself.

Imagine no one can give you advice. What would you do?

Over time, you'll begin to understand that your own decisions are more valuable than others' opinions.

What Will You Gain When You Learn to Rely on Yourself?

You will become more confident and stop depending on others' opinions. You won't be afraid of change because you'll know that you can handle any situation. You'll begin making decisions without fear of judgment and will feel comfortable, even if someone disagrees with you.

But most importantly, you'll realize that you can always count on yourself. You are already managing, and you can do even more. Just allow yourself to recognize that strength.

CHAPTER 13
BUILDING A NEW LIFE

You've done an immense amount of work. The difficult period when you learned to recognize your worth, trust yourself, set boundaries, and handle everything on your own is behind you. You didn't just leave an abusive relationship — you've started changing your life. The final step remains — to build it the way you want it.

You're at the finish line. Imagine that ahead of you is not just "a new chapter," but the opportunity to create a life where you feel truly comfortable. A life where there's no place for fear, humiliation, or the constant feeling that you're "not good enough." Now, you are the one deciding what kind of environment you want to be in, what you want to do, and which principles will define your path.

It's important to understand that building a new life is not about sudden resetting or completely erasing the past. Your experience, even painful, is a part of your story. But now, you can choose which lessons to carry with you and what to leave behind. It's not about forgetting everything that happened, but about building your reality on new, healthy foundations.

But where to begin? How to stop looking back and move forward with confidence? Let's go over the key points that will help you create a life full of more joy, confidence, and freedom.

DEFINING WHAT YOU WANT FROM LIFE

After leaving toxic relationships, you are faced with a new life. But what it will look like depends on you. It's important not just to move on but to consciously choose what you want.

In Chapter 10, we already discussed how to define your desires, values, and dreams. Now, you have the chance to create a life that brings you joy and fulfillment. The main thing is not to be afraid to ask yourself questions and seek answers.

CREATING AN ENVIRONMENT THAT SUPPORTS YOU

When starting a new life, your social circle often changes. This can happen naturally — as you start valuing yourself, people who used to exploit your vulnerability may disappear from your life. Sometimes, this is painful, but in reality, it's a cleansing — freeing yourself from those who bring nothing good into your life. Let's discuss how to create an environment around you that helps you grow and feel safe.

1. Audit Your Environment

To begin, you need to understand who is currently in your life and how these people affect you.

Take a piece of paper or open your notes and write down the names of people you often interact with. These could be friends, colleagues, relatives — anyone who has an influence on your emotional state.

Next to each name, write down what kind of feelings this person evokes in you.

- *Who supports and inspires you?*
- *Who listens and respects your boundaries?*
- *Who makes you feel guilty without reason?*
- *Who devalues your experiences?*
- *Who uses you for their own benefit?*

This practice will help you consciously look at your

environment and understand which relationships energize you and which ones drain you.

2. Recognizing Toxic People

Not all relationships bring joy and support. Sometimes we interact with people simply out of habit, not realizing how they are gradually undermining our confidence.

How to know if someone in your life is toxic? Pay attention to the following signs:

- *Guilt:* After interacting with this person, you feel guilty even if you did nothing wrong.
- *Constant criticism and devaluation:* They may say, "You always overdo it," "You're too sensitive," "You'll never succeed."
- *Emotional exhaustion:* Communicating with this person drains you instead of bringing joy.
- *Ignoring your boundaries:* If you say something makes you uncomfortable but the person continues to act the same way, it's a warning sign.

Toxic people can't always be immediately removed from your life, especially if they are relatives or colleagues. But you can minimize communication or clearly set boundaries (as discussed in Chapter 8 on boundaries).

3. Finding People Who Will Inspire You

If your social circle has changed (shrunk), it's important not to isolate yourself but to consciously seek out new people with whom you will feel comfortable.

How to expand your social circle?

- Try interest-based communities. Find clubs, courses, or events where like-minded people gather.
- Look at the people already in your life. Perhaps among your acquaintances, there are people with whom you've always enjoyed spending time but didn't pay enough attention to.
- Allow yourself to be open. After leaving toxic relationships,

you might want to close yourself off from the world. But if you want to find support, it's important to give people a chance. Prioritize quality over quantity. It's better to have one or two reliable friends than dozens of superficial contacts.

4. Building Healthy Relationships

When you find new people, it's important not to repeat old patterns. If in the past, you were used to being accommodating, sacrificing yourself for others, now it's essential to build relationships differently.

How to know if new relationships are healthy?

- *You can be yourself:* You don't have to pretend to be stronger, happier, or more accommodating than you truly are.
- *Your boundaries are respected:* If you say "no," it's accepted without pressure or manipulation.
- *There's reciprocity:* You don't just give; you receive support in return.
- *You feel comfortable:* After spending time with this person, you feel energized and happy, not drained.

Your environment plays a huge role in your recovery. You no longer have to tolerate those who cause you pain or use you. Now, you can choose who will be in your life.

Remember: it's better to be alone than in an environment that breaks you. But if you open yourself to the world, you will undoubtedly find people who see your true worth.

HOW TO OVERCOME THE FEAR OF NEW RELATIONSHIPS

After toxic experiences, any new interaction — romantic, friendly, or professional — may feel risky. You already know what it's like to be deceived, used, or suppressed. Now, your psyche is doing everything to protect you from potential pain: distrust, unwarranted caution, and sometimes even the desire to shut yourself off from people altogether.

But it's important to understand: fear is not a sign that you can't trust someone else. It's simply a reminder of past experiences. It doesn't have to control your life. You've already learned to recognize warning signs and set boundaries. Now, you need to learn to let healthy relationships into your life.

You may feel scared, thinking you'll choose the wrong person again or find yourself in unhealthy relationships once more. But let's remember why this is unlikely:

- *You recognize your value:* You will no longer tolerate what once seemed normal.
- *You know how to spot manipulation:* Now, you know that words and actions must align, and apologies without action mean nothing.
- *You set boundaries:* If someone tries to cross them, you'll notice and be able to respond.
- *You no longer seek confirmation of your worth from others:* You are no longer dependent on others' opinions, which makes you less vulnerable to toxic people.

All of this, of course, doesn't make you fully invulnerable to repeating past scenarios. Yes, you can still make mistakes — just like anyone else — but now you have the tools to recognize warning signals in time.

Alongside fear, you may feel anxious about whether your new relationships are truly healthy. In this case, focus on feelings and facts. Here are signs to help you distinguish healthy relationships from potentially toxic ones:

- People see you as a person, not a resource. They respect you not for what you give, but for who you are.
- Your boundaries are respected. If you say "no," no one tries to convince you otherwise or make you feel guilty.
- You feel calm and safe. There's no need to constantly guess the other person's mood, fear their reactions, or adjust to them.

- You can be yourself. You don't have to hide your emotions, feel ashamed of your vulnerability, or play a role to be accepted.
- There's reciprocity. The relationship is built on respect and support, not one-sided compromises.

If, in a new relationship, you feel anxiety, discomfort, or uncertainty — don't ignore those feelings. They may be signs that something is off.

Also, after leaving abusive relationships, you might feel the need to "check" every person, analyze their behavior, look for hidden motives, or even control. This is normal, but it's important not to fall into extremes and shut yourself off from everyone.

Don't rush. Let relationships develop naturally, without pressure or haste. You don't have to trust immediately, but don't push people away just because of fear of another abusive situation.

Trust your feelings. If someone triggers anxiety or discomfort, it's a reason to think. If someone makes you feel calm and easy — it could be a healthy connection.

Give yourself time to adapt. At first, any close relationship might scare you. It doesn't mean you should avoid them, but you can proceed gradually.

Remember: you're no longer a victim. Now, you choose who will be in your life and who won't. You have the right to close the door on those who don't bring peace and joy into your life.

New relationships aren't just about love. They're about friends, colleagues, a new environment. You're learning to build your life anew, and yes, it can be scary. But now you have the knowledge, awareness, and inner support to create healthy connections.

You are no longer the person you were before. You won't make the same mistakes again. Now, you're building your life the way you want.

HOW TO BUILD A STABLE FUTURE?

Creating a new life after leaving a toxic relationship is not just about emotions, self-esteem, and your environment—it's also about practical aspects. Learning to live anew means not only restoring your emotional balance but also building a strong foundation for your future.

Maybe your life used to be chaotic: constant stress, lack of financial control, no career planning. Now it's time to take responsibility for your life and make it stable.

Financial stability is one of the key aspects that helps you feel confident and secure. If you were once dependent on a partner, parents, or others, it's now crucial to establish your own financial foundation.

Where to Start?

- *Analyze your current financial situation.* Make a list of your income and expenses to understand how much you need for a comfortable life.
- *Determine what steps will help you become financially independent.* Do you need to improve your qualifications, change jobs, or learn to manage your budget?
- *Start saving money.* Even a small financial cushion can create a sense of stability and security.
- *Explore new income opportunities.* This could be a side job, freelancing, or learning a new profession.

This is important because financial independence gives you the freedom to choose. You won't have to stay in a relationship or job that destroys you just because you're afraid of being left without money.

Since work takes up a significant part of life, it's important that it brings not only income but also satisfaction. If you used to accept any job just to please someone or avoid conflict, now you can ask yourself: What do I truly want to do?

Here are some tips to help you find your dream job:
- *Assess your skills and strengths.* What are you good at? What makes you feel confident?
- *Think about careers you liked in the past.* Maybe you've always wanted to be creative, work with people, or develop in a field you once abandoned.
- *Don't be afraid to learn.* If you feel you lack the necessary knowledge or experience, that's okay. The world is constantly changing, and new skills can be learned at any age.
- *Set career goals.* For example, find a new job within six months, take a course, or increase your income by a certain amount.

When you have a job you love — or at least a clear understanding of your career direction — you feel more confident. You know you can rely on yourself and that your future is in your own hands.

CREATING A SAFE SPACE

Emotional peace is impossible without a sense of security. It's important to create a space where you can recharge, feel safe, and not fear that someone will violate your boundaries again.

How to create your own space?
- *Set up a place where you feel comfortable.* This could be your own apartment, a room, or even a small space you can call your own.
- *Make your surroundings cozy.* Your home should be a place of restoration. Add things that bring you joy—books, flowers, candles, art, music. Make it a place you love returning to.
- *Develop safety rituals.* If you feel anxious, think about what makes you feel secure—strong locks, an alarm system, the support of friends, or even self-defense skills.

- *Avoid places and people that remind you of the past.* If something triggers bad memories and anxiety, allow yourself to let it go.

When you have your own place in the world, you feel more grounded. You know there's a space where no one will harm you, where you can relax and recover.

A stable future is not something distant and unattainable — it's the result of your conscious decisions. When you have financial independence, fulfilling work, and a safe space, you are no longer dependent on others' opinions, you are not afraid of loneliness, and you know you can handle any challenges.

You've already come a long way. The final step is to build a life where you feel good. And now, you have all the tools to make it happen.

FINAL WORD

You've come a long way. From the first realizations, doubts, and questions to a deep understanding of yourself, your boundaries, and the life you truly want to live. This journey may not have been easy, and some chapters were hard to get through. But you kept moving forward. And that's the most important proof that you have the strength to change your life.

Right now, you're on the threshold of a new chapter — a chapter that you're writing yourself. Without pressure and imposed beliefs. Now you know how to recognize abuse, how to protect your boundaries, how to not lose yourself in relationships, and how to build a life where there is room for respect, love, and personal choice.

If at any moment you find it hard, know this: you've already proven that you can handle it. You've already won, because you found the strength within yourself to see the truth and begin changing your life.

And even though there is more of the journey ahead, it's now different — it's not a path of survival, but a path to yourself, to awareness, to a happy and fulfilling life.

I sincerely believe in you. You deserve better. And you can achieve it. ♥

With love and support,
your Julianna Kent

WORKBOOK

Welcome to the 30-Day Recovery Workbook!

This workbook is designed to assist those who have decided to go through the recovery process after leaving an abusive relationship on their own. Here, you will find both familiar exercises from the book and completely new tasks, developed specifically for the 30-day recovery program.

This is your personal assistant that will help you understand yourself more deeply, process emotions, release old beliefs, and move forward.

HOW IS THIS WORKBOOK STRUCTURED?

It's designed for 30 days, but this is not a strict schedule. You can go at your own pace, dwell on topics that are important to you, or come back to exercises later. Some tasks might immediately resonate with you, while others might seem difficult or irrelevant — and that's fine. If you feel strong resistance, try asking yourself, "Why is this exercise difficult for me?" but if it doesn't fit at all — just skip it.

The key is not to strive for perfect execution of all the tasks, but to use them as a tool to help you understand yourself better and heal.

HOW TO WORK WITH THIS WORKBOOK?

- Be honest with yourself. No one but you will see these entries, so allow yourself to be sincere.

- Don't rush. This is not a race. Go through the exercises at the pace that feels comfortable for you.
- Progress is not only about the result, but also the process itself. Even if it seems like you're not making progress, you are still moving forward.

WORKBOOK STRUCTURE

This workbook is divided into four weeks, each dedicated to an important stage of recovery.

Week 1: Recognizing and Accepting Your Emotions

Your emotional state after leaving an abusive relationship can be chaotic: pain, anxiety, anger, doubt. This week will help you sort through your emotions, learn to recognize them, and process them in a healthy way.

- Identifying which emotions are connected to your experience.
- Learning to listen to yourself and distinguish healthy from toxic reactions.
- Understanding feelings of guilt, fear, and anger and learning to accept them.

Week 2: Setting Boundaries and Healthy Habits

Without boundaries, it's impossible to build a healthy life. If you've allowed others to control you and your life, this week will help you learn how to say "no" and protect your personal space.

- Learning to set boundaries in all areas of life.
- Working on preventing a return to destructive relationships.
- Forming habits that help you care for yourself.

▉ Week 3: Restoring Self-Esteem and Confidence

Abuse destroys your sense of self-worth. This week is aimed at helping you regain your confidence and believe in yourself again.

- Recognizing the impact of abuse on your self-esteem.
- Learning to see your strengths and rely on them.
- Practicing techniques to reduce self-criticism and the negative inner voice.

▉ Week 4: Creating a Vision of a Healthy Future

Recovery is not just about getting out of abuse; it's about creating a new life. In the final week, you will begin to consciously build your future and fill it with what truly matters to you.

- Defining what we want in the future.
- Learning to see yourself outside the role of a victim and build healthy relationships.
- Creating a strategy for how to build a life filled with joy, not pain.

You've already started moving forward by deciding to change your life. Now, let's keep moving forward!

WEEK 1: RECOGNIZING AND ACCEPTING YOUR EMOTIONS

Welcome to the first week of recovery.

This week is dedicated to the most important step — understanding your emotions. You might experience pain, fear, anger, resentment, fatigue, disappointment, or even emptiness. And that's okay.

Emotional abuse teaches us to ignore our feelings, devalue them, or be afraid to express them. But accepting these feelings is the first step towards processing them.

Throughout this week, you will observe your emotions, learn to recognize them, record them, and understand them. This will help separate your true feelings from the beliefs imposed on you and start to see the bigger picture more clearly.

DAY 1: WHAT AM I FEELING RIGHT NOW?

Today, your task is to simply stop and honestly answer the question: "What am I feeling right now?"

Write everything down, even if it seems insignificant. Sometimes we think we "should" feel a certain way, but what really matters is this — your true emotions.

📌 Exercise:

1. Close your eyes, take a deep breath, and ask yourself: *"How do I feel?"*

_____
_____
_____
_____
_____
_____
_____
_____
_____

2. Write down everything that comes to mind. For example:
- *I feel anxious because...*
- *I am angry because...*
- *I feel sad because...*
- *I feel empty, but I don't know why...*

_____
_____
_____
_____
_____
_____
_____
_____

3. If it's hard to express your emotions, try naming at least three words that describe your state.

_____
_____
_____
_____
_____
_____
_____
_____
_____
_____
_____
_____

Remember: there are no right or wrong emotions. Your task is to notice them and allow them to exist.

DAY 2: WHERE DO I FEEL EMOTIONS IN MY BODY?

Our emotions are not just in our heads — they live in our bodies. Anxiety can feel like tension in the shoulders, fear — like tightness in the chest, sadness — like heaviness in the stomach.

📌 Exercise:

Sit in a quiet place, close your eyes, and focus on your body.

Do a "scan" from the top of your head to the tips of your fingers and record:

- Where do you feel tension?

_____
_____
_____
_____
_____

- Where do you feel heaviness?

_____
_____
_____
_____
_____

- Is there any tightness, discomfort, or trembling?

_____
_____
_____
_____

Identify which emotion is linked to this sensation.

Write: "I feel _____ in my _____ part of the body."

It's important: This exercise helps you understand how your emotions affect your physical state and learn to recognize them.

DAY 3: WHAT WAS I TOLD ABOUT MY EMOTIONS?

When we were growing up, we were often told how we "should" feel:

"Don't be sad, you're strong!"

"You're too sensitive, don't dramatize!"

"Relax, it's not that bad!"

These words make us doubt our feelings and suppress them.

📌 Exercise:
1. Recall phrases from childhood or past relationships that made you distrust your feelings.
2. Write them down and try to rephrase them into supportive words. For example:

- *"You're too sensitive"*   *"I have the right to feel the way I feel."*
- *"Don't get angry, it's not pretty"*   *"My anger is valid."*

_____
_____
_____
_____
_____
_____
_____
_____
_____
_____
_____
_____
_____
_____

Conclusion: Your emotions are a part of you. They don't require anyone else's approval.

DAY 4: DO I ALLOW MYSELF TO FEEL?

Abusive relationships force us to suppress our emotions, as expressing them may lead to criticism or punishment.

📌 Exercise:

1. Imagine your emotions are guests. Which emotions do you allow to "enter the house," and which do you ignore?
2. Write down:
- Which emotions do you allow yourself to feel?
- Which do you suppress?
- Why?
3. Try allowing yourself to feel one emotion you usually suppress.

_____
_____
_____
_____
_____
_____
_____
_____
_____
_____
_____
_____
_____
_____
_____
_____

It's important: There are no "bad" emotions. All of them have meaning and the right to exist.

DAY 5: HOW DO MY EMOTIONS AFFECT MY LIFE?

Sometimes we don't realize how suppressed emotions control our decisions.

📌 Exercise:

1. Complete the table:

Emotion	When do I feel it?	How does it affect my actions?
Anxiety	Before an important conversation	I delay making a decision, avoid dialogue
Anger	When I am ignored	I shut down or, on the contrary, explode
Sadness	When I feel lonely	I lose motivation, refuse to interact

2. Make a conclusion: *How do emotions control you? How can you react differently?*

_____

_____

_____

_____

_____

_____

_____

_____

_____

Task: Learn to see the connection between feelings and behavior.

DAY 6: HOW WOULD I DESCRIBE MY EMOTIONS TO A CLOSE FRIEND?

Sometimes we are strict with ourselves, but supportive to others.

📌 Exercise:
1. Imagine that your friend is feeling the same emotions as you right now.
2. Write a letter of support to yourself as if you were writing to a friend.

_____

_____

_____

_____

_____

_____

_____

_____

_____

_____

_____

_____

_____

_____

_____

_____

_____

_____

_____

Conclusion: You deserve the same support that you give to others.

DAY 7: END OF WEEK REVIEW

After completing the exercises, it's important not just to move forward, but to reflect on your responses. Read your entries again and ask yourself a few questions:

1. What did you learn about your emotions?
2. What discoveries did you make?
3. What was difficult, and what was helpful?

_____
_____
_____
_____
_____
_____
_____
_____
_____
_____
_____
_____
_____
_____
_____
_____
_____
_____
_____

🍃 Next week is dedicated to setting boundaries. Now that you have a better understanding of your emotions, it's time to learn how to protect yourself.

You're doing great. Keep moving forward. 🚀

WEEK 2: SETTING BOUNDARIES AND HEALTHY HABITS

Congratulations! You've already done a tremendous amount of work. You've started to understand your emotions, and now it's time to take the next step — setting boundaries to protect yourself from further emotional abuse.

Boundaries are not walls, but doors. They don't shut you off from the world but allow you to choose who to let into your life and who not to.

This week, we will:

✓ Learn to say "no" without guilt

✓ Develop healthy habits that help maintain inner stability in different situations

✓ Identify moments when your boundaries are crossed and learn how to respond

Every day, you will take a small step toward living in a world where you are respected, and where you respect yourself.

DAY 8: WHERE ARE MY BOUNDARIES?

Have you ever noticed that sometimes you agree to things you don't like just to avoid conflict? If your answer is yes, it means your boundaries are blurry.

📌 Exercise:

1. Recall the last three instances when you did something against your will because you didn't want to hurt someone, were afraid to refuse, or felt pressured.
2. Write down:
- *What happened?*
- *Why did you agree?*
- *How did you feel afterward?*
3. Now imagine you could calmly say "no." *What would you say? How would the situation change?*

_____
_____
_____
_____
_____
_____
_____
_____
_____
_____
_____
_____
_____
_____
_____
_____
_____
_____
_____
_____
_____
_____
_____
_____

Conclusion: You will see that your refusal would not lead to a catastrophe. The person would either accept your boundaries, find another solution, or perhaps be slightly offended but eventually calm down.

You will also realize that the discomfort from refusal is temporary, but agreeing against your will leaves an unpleasant aftertaste for a long time.

The more you understand that "no" is not rudeness but self-care, the easier it will be to defend your boundaries.

DAY 9: "NO" WITHOUT GUILT

Why is it so difficult for us to say no? Guilt, fear of disappointing someone, and fear of conflict — all of these make us say "yes" when we want to say "no."

📌 Exercise:
1. Recall a situation where it was hard for you to refuse.
2. Imagine you can say "no" calmly and confidently. Write your ideal refusal phrase.
3. Try using it in real life at least once in the next few days.

_____
_____
_____
_____
_____
_____
_____
_____
_____
_____
_____
_____
_____
_____
_____
_____
_____
_____

Important: You have the right to refuse without explanations and justifications.

DAY 10: WHO REGULARLY CROSSES MY BOUNDARIES?

Some people cross our boundaries accidentally. Others do it systematically. It's important to understand the difference.

📌 Exercise:

1. Write down the names of three people who most often make you do things that make you uncomfortable.
2. Determine:

- Do they do this consciously, or are they just unaware?
- How do you usually react?
- How could you respond differently next time?

_____

_____

_____

_____

_____

_____

_____

_____

_____

_____

_____

_____

_____

_____

_____

_____

_____

_____

Conclusion: Sometimes, simply stating your boundaries is enough to improve the situation.

DAY 11: WHAT TO DO IF MY BOUNDARIES ARE CROSSED?

📌 Exercise:
1. Write down three situations in which someone disrespected your boundaries.
2. Come up with a calm but firm response that would put the person in their place.
3. Remember this simple structure:
- Describe the situation (*"I noticed that you interrupt me in meetings."*)
- State your boundary (*"I want to be listened to until I finish."*)
- Clearly state what will happen next (*"If you continue, I will end the conversation."*)

_____
_____
_____
_____
_____
_____
_____
_____
_____
_____
_____
_____
_____
_____
_____
_____
_____
_____

Important: Your boundaries are your responsibility.

DAY 12: HEALTHY HABITS THAT STRENGTHEN BOUNDARIES

When you feel tired and vulnerable, protecting boundaries becomes harder. That's why it's important to create habits that give you strength.

📌 Exercise:

1. Write down three things that give you a sense of confidence. These can be sports, yoga, walks, reading, good music.
2. Choose one habit that you will start practicing daily.

_____

_____

_____

_____

_____

_____

_____

_____

_____

_____

_____

_____

_____

_____

_____

_____

_____

_____

_____

Conclusion: Self-care helps you maintain inner stability.

DAY 13: PEOPLE WHO RESPECT MY BOUNDARIES

Boundaries are not only about protection. They are also about those close to you who respect you.

📌 Exercise:

1. Write down two or three people with whom you feel comfortable because they don't cross your boundaries.
2. Think about: How are these relationships different from toxic ones?
3. How can you strengthen these relationships and spend more time with these people?

_____
_____
_____
_____
_____
_____
_____
_____
_____
_____
_____
_____
_____
_____
_____
_____
_____
_____

Important: Respectful relationships help us regain confidence in ourselves.

DAY 14: WEEK SUMMARY

Read your entries (exercises 8-13) again and ask yourself a few questions:

1. How has your attitude towards boundaries changed?
2. What was the most difficult part?
3. Which step would you like to reinforce in your life?

_____
_____
_____
_____
_____
_____
_____
_____
_____
_____
_____
_____
_____
_____
_____
_____

Next week will be dedicated to self-esteem and confidence. It's time to learn to accept yourself and believe in your worth.

You're doing great. Keep moving forward. 🚀

WEEK 3: RESTORING SELF-ESTEEM AND CONFIDENCE

You've already done a great deal of work, learning to recognize your emotions and set boundaries. Now it's time to focus on another important aspect — restoring your self-esteem, which often suffers in toxic relationships.

When you were constantly criticized, devalued, and made to doubt yourself, you might have started believing that you're not good enough. These thoughts are not yours. They are the result of the experiences you've been through. But you can rewrite your story.

This week, we will:

✓ Break down negative beliefs about ourselves
✓ Learn to recognize our strengths
✓ Build confidence and independence

Every day — a small step toward restoring yourself.

DAY 15: WHAT DO I THINK ABOUT MYSELF?

Your self-esteem is made up of the thoughts you repeat about yourself. Sometimes these thoughts are so automatic that we don't even notice how they control us.

📌 Exercise:

1. Write down 5-7 phrases that you most often say to yourself (even mentally). For example:
- *"I'm not good enough"*
- *"I won't succeed"*
- *"I'm too sensitive"*
2. Now ask yourself: *Where did these thoughts come from? Who first told you these things?*
3. Write next to each phrase: *"Is this true, or was this implanted in me?"*

_____

_____
_____
_____
_____
_____
_____
_____
_____
_____
_____
_____
_____
_____
_____
_____
_____
_____
_____
_____

Important: Most negative thoughts are not your voice. They are the voice of those who once made you doubt yourself.

DAY 16: HOW DO OTHERS PERCEIVE ME?

Sometimes our perception of ourselves does not match how others see us.

📌 Exercise:
1. Write 5 words you would use to describe yourself.
2. Ask three people who love you how they would describe you.
3. Compare the answers. What was unexpected?

_____
_____
_____
_____
_____
_____
_____
_____
_____
_____
_____
_____
_____
_____
_____
_____
_____
_____
_____
_____

Conclusion: You may see yourself worse than you really are.

DAY 17: ACHIEVEMENTS I FORGET

In moments when our self-esteem is low, we think we don't know how to do anything or accomplish anything. But this is not true.

📌 Exercise:

1. Write down 10 things you've been proud of. They can be big or small achievements:

- *Completed an important project*
- *Managed to get through a tough period*
- *Supported a friend in a difficult time*
- *Chose yourself over toxic relationships*

2. Highlight the three points that are most important to you.

_____
_____
_____
_____
_____
_____
_____
_____
_____
_____
_____
_____
_____
_____
_____
_____
_____
_____

Important: You are stronger than you think.

DAY 18: INNER CRITIC VS. INNER FRIEND

Abuse creates in us a harsh inner critic who is never satisfied. Let's try to switch the voice in our head to one of support.

📌 Exercise:
1. Recall the last time you criticized yourself. Write down that thought.
2. Now imagine that this isn't directed at you, but at your friend. What would you say to support them?
3. Write down that response and read it whenever you want to criticize yourself.

_____

_____

_____

_____

_____

_____

_____

_____

_____

_____

_____

_____

_____

_____

_____

_____

_____

_____

_____

Conclusion: You deserve the same support you give to others.

DAY 19: COMPLIMENTS TO MYSELF

Abusive relationships make us depend on others' opinions. Today, we will learn to notice the good in ourselves without outside validation.

📌 Exercise:
1. Write 5 compliments to yourself (if it's hard, imagine you're saying them to your friend).
2. Say them out loud in front of the mirror, looking yourself in the eye.

_____
_____
_____
_____
_____
_____
_____
_____
_____
_____
_____
_____
_____
_____
_____
_____

Important: Your voice about yourself matters more than others' words.

DAY 20: HOW AM I DIFFERENT FROM MY PAST SELF?

You change every day. Sometimes the changes are subtle, but that doesn't mean they're not happening.

📌 Exercise:

1. Recall yourself a year ago. What were you like?
2. In what ways have you become stronger, wiser, or more confident?
3. Write down 3 things you did back then but no longer do (for example, tolerate insults, be afraid to say "no").

_____

_____

_____

_____

_____

_____

_____

_____

_____

_____

_____

_____

_____

_____

_____

_____

_____

_____

Conclusion: You're already growing and moving forward.

DAY 21: WEEK SUMMARY

Read your entries (exercises 8-13) again and ask yourself a few questions:

1. How has your perception of yourself changed over the week?
2. What exercises were the most difficult?
3. What step do you want to continue practicing?

_____

_____

_____

_____

_____

_____

_____

_____

_____

_____

_____

_____

_____

_____

_____

_____

_____

_____

_____

_____

Next week will be dedicated to creating a healthy future. Now that you know how to protect yourself, it's time to think about what you really want from life.

You're on the right track. Keep moving forward. 🚀

WEEK 4: CREATING A VISION OF A HEALTHY FUTURE

Congratulations! You've already come a long way — you've understood your emotions, learned to recognize your worth, and set boundaries. Now it's time to move forward and build a future where you will feel free, safe, and happy.

This week, we will:

✓ Define who you want to be in the future

✓ Learn to dream without the limitations imposed by the abuser

✓ Take real steps for positive changes in life

DAY 22: WHO DO I WANT TO BE?

📌 Exercise:

1. Imagine that one year from now, you wake up in the morning. *You are happy, confident, and there are no toxic people in your life. How do you look? How do you feel? Where do you live? What are you doing?*

2. Write down how you want to be in one year — what words would you use to describe yourself? For example:

- *I am calm and confident in myself*
- *I know how to set boundaries*
- *I am surrounded by people who respect me*

_____

_____

_____

_____

_____

_____

_____

_____

_____

_____

Important: When you clearly envision your goal, it becomes easier to move towards it.

DAY 23: WHAT DO I WANT IN LIFE?

📌 Exercise:
1. Write down 5 things you want to change or improve in your life. These can be any areas: personal relationships, career, health, self-confidence.
2. For each of these areas, answer the question: What small steps can I take right now to move towards these changes?

_____

_____

_____

_____

_____

_____

_____

_____

_____

_____

_____

_____

_____

_____

_____

_____

_____

_____

_____

Conclusion: The future is created through small actions, not just one decision.

Day 24: How to Choose an Environment that Supports Me?

📌 Exercise:
1. Write down a list of people who support you and with whom you feel comfortable.
2. Write down a list of those with whom you feel suppressed, tense, or guilty.
3. How can you spend more time with the first group and limit communication with the second?

_____
_____
_____
_____
_____
_____
_____
_____
_____
_____
_____
_____
_____
_____
_____
_____
_____
_____
_____

Important: You have the right to choose whom you communicate with, and your environment directly affects your self-esteem.

DAY 25: DO I ALLOW MYSELF TO BE HAPPY?

📌 Exercise:

1. Imagine that happiness is your natural setting. But do you have internal restrictions on happiness?

2. Write down:

- *What are you afraid of if you become happy? (For example, "What if I start living better, and my close ones judge me?")*
- *What beliefs are holding you back? ("I must earn happiness first" or "If I'm happy, something will go wrong")*

3. Write down new beliefs to replace the old ones. For example:

- *I have the right to be happy simply because I live.*
- *My happiness doesn't depend on others.*

_____

_____

_____

_____

_____

_____

_____

_____

_____

_____

_____

_____

_____

_____

_____

_____

_____

Conclusion: You can allow yourself to feel joy right now.

DAY 26: HOW TO FORM NEW HABITS?

📌 Exercise:

1. Choose one habit that will help you feel better (for example, walking, journaling, reading before bed).
2. Determine a small step that will make it easy to implement (for example, writing just one sentence in your journal each day).
3. Think of a way to remind yourself of it (set a reminder, link it to another habit, such as drinking tea and writing in your journal).

_____

_____

_____

_____

_____

_____

_____

_____

_____

_____

_____

_____

_____

_____

_____

_____

_____

_____

_____

_____

Conclusion: Small steps lead to big changes.

DAY 27: HOW TO FIND JOY IN THE PRESENT?

📌 Exercise:
1. Write down 5 things you are grateful for right now.
2. What are the three things that bring you joy every day?
3. What can you do from what you've written today to feel the pleasure of life?

_____

_____

_____

_____

_____

_____

_____

_____

_____

_____

_____

_____

_____

_____

_____

_____

_____

_____

_____

_____

_____

Important: Happiness is not in the future, it starts with the "now."

DAY 28: HOW TO LET GO OF THE PAST?

📌 Exercise:

1. Write a letter to your past self, who was in an abusive relationship.
2. Tell them what you know now that you didn't know back then.
3. Thank yourself for choosing the path to healing.

_____
_____
_____
_____
_____
_____
_____
_____
_____
_____
_____
_____
_____
_____
_____
_____
_____
_____
_____
_____

Conclusion: The past doesn't define you. You are already different.

DAY 29: HOW TO SOLIDIFY THE RESULTS?

📌 Exercise:
1. Look at what you wrote on the first day. What has changed since then?
2. What do you want to continue doing after the program ends?
3. Write down 3 things that will help you avoid returning to toxic relationships.

_____

_____

_____

_____

_____

_____

_____

_____

_____

_____

_____

_____

_____

_____

_____

_____

_____

_____

_____

Important: Recovery is a process, but you've already made significant progress.

DAY 30: PROGRAM SUMMARY

Today is the last day of working with the workbook, and it's a wonderful moment to look back and evaluate your journey.

Review:

Take some time to reread your entries from the past few weeks. Pay attention to the changes in your thoughts, emotions, and self-perception. Answer a few questions:

- *What has changed in me over these 30 days?*
- *Which exercises were most helpful for me?*
- *What have I learned about myself?*
- *What steps am I ready to take next for my growth and recovery?*

_____

_____

_____

_____

_____

_____

_____

This self-work doesn't end today — it continues, but now you have an understanding of how to move forward. Celebrate the path you've walked, and remember that every conscious action brings you closer to the life you deserve.

This is not the end, but the beginning of a new life. You've made it. Now you know how to protect yourself, respect your boundaries, and move forward.

You are stronger than you think. And you deserve the best.